ARMOUR
NEVER
WEARIES

Armour Never Wearies

Scale and Lamellar Armour in the West, from the Bronze Age to the 19th Century

Timothy Dawson

Men soon grow sick of battle; when Zeus the steward of warfare tilts the scales, and cold steel reaps the fields, the grain is very little but the straw is very much. The belly is a bad mourner, and fasting will not bury the dead. Too many are falling, man after man and day after day; how could one ever have a moment's rest from privations? No, we must harden our hearts, and bury the man who dies and shed our tears that day. But those who survive the horrors of war should not forget to eat and drink, and then we shall be better able to wear our armour, which never grows weary, and to fight our enemies for ever and ever.

The Iliad, Book 19

Cover illustrations. *Front*: A cavalryman from the *Stuttgart Psalter*. (Würtenburg State Library) *Back*: Polish *karacena* parade armour. (Polish Army Museum, Warsaw)

First published 2013
by Spellmount, an imprint of The History Press
The Mill, Brimscombe Port
Stroud, Gloucestershire, GL5 2QG
www.thehistorypress.co.uk

British Library Cataloguing in Publication Data.
A catalogue record for this book is available from the British Library.

ISBN 978 0 7524 8862 2

Typesetting and origination by The History Press
Printed in Great Britain

Eyam Book Barn
@ Eyam Hall Craft Centre

ARMOUR NEVER WEARIES

WED 03 JULY 2019

for secondhand books, CDs, DVDs and jigsaw puzzles

A community bookshop raising
money for local
organisations and projects

Opening Times

Providing volunteers are available
we are open

Wednesday 11.00am—4.00pm

Thursday   11.00am—4.00pm

Saturday   11.00am—4.00pm

Sunday   11.00am—4.00pm

Bank Holidays 12.00am-3.00pm

Open extra days during school
holidays

Eyam Hall Craft Centre
Church Street
Eyam
S32 5QW

07707 059154

eyambookbarn@gmail.com
facebook: Eyam Book Barn

CONTENTS

ACKNOWLEDGEMENTS

The author would like to to thank Michel Dziewulski of the National Museum in Krakow and Karen Watts of the Royal Armouries Museum for facilitating access to items in their respective collections; Donald LaRocca of the Metropolitan Museum for invaluable references and clarification of unpublished details of items in that collection; Mamuka Tsutsumia for providing information on Eastern European finds; and Nadeem Ahmad for useful discussion.

About the author

Timothy Dawson's interest in medieval history, and especially military history and that of the Near East, was initially fostered by his participation in historical recreation ('re-enactment') and public education. Such interests led him to a career as a history educator and historical craftsman. He took a BA in Classical Studies at the University of Melbourne, Australia, followed by a doctorate at the University of New England (New South Wales, Australia). He has published widely on aspects of material culture and social history, particularly clothing and military matters, using a methodology which combines conventional scholarship with practical experience and reconstruction to make significant advances in certain areas. Timothy is the author of *Byzantine Cavalryman: Eastern Roman Empire, c.900–1204* and *Byzantine Infantryman: Eastern Roman Empire, c.900–1204* for Osprey Publishing and *One Thousand Years of Lamellar Construction in the Roman World*, Levantia Guides no. 8.

INTRODUCTION

The question of whether men first contrived protective equipment for themselves to defend against beasts they set out to hunt, or whether it was the result of conflict arising between human communities, is likely to remain a mystery. What is beyond doubt is that once the need for such protection was perceived, the earliest manufactured form must have been small pieces of naturally occurring durable material, horn and bone, bound together with textiles or leather to create a fabric. This volume sets out to gather the hitherto dispersed evidence for external small plate armours as they were used in the West, to illustrate the permutations in form, and trace the fluctuating patterns of usage.

In defining 'the West', I use the conventional border of the line of the Ural Mountains, the 60° East meridian. This will, admittedly, take in areas that many people might not think of as 'Western', such as Iran and Arabia, but the former is certainly fitting, because external small plate armours were central to its military practices for a very long period of time, and because of the significant influence that region exerted on Mediterranean and Near Eastern societies in early times. The reason for the geographic restriction is primarily linguistic. It is very much harder for me to access source material from the Far East. The restriction is not absolute, however. From time to time I will refer to Oriental material for the sake of comparison where that is useful.

In its final realisation, the temporal parameters of this project have ended up being rather wider than anticipated. The starting point in the Bronze Age was noted by earlier scholars, and nothing has arisen in the last few decades to alter that. Rather unexpected, though, was the discovery that scale armour, at least, remained in functional military use much later than I imagined, beyond the middle of the nineteenth century. An epilogue to that is the use of scale armour in theatre and other pastimes, which brings us to the start of the twentieth century.

Origins of the armour

The origins of external small plate armour are lost in prehistory. While scale armour begins in very elementary form and becomes more sophisticated over time, the very earliest surviving examples of lamellar and its representations already appear in sophisticated forms from the outset. That those early sophisticated forms do not survive and spread implies they they did not necessarily have a considerable prior history involving gradual technological development, but perhaps were localised products of some unusually inspired artisan or group. Lamellar is often thought to have been introduced to the West from Central Asia in Late Antiquity, yet in 1967 H. Russell Robinson observed that the earliest evidence for lamellar is actually found in the West. This observation still holds true, despite all the research and archaeology that has been carried out since, with lamellar not reaching the Far East until Late Antiquity. Decades earlier, Bengt Thordeman felt able to be much more definite, writing that the evidence 'proves that lamellar construction originated in the Near East'.[1] With all due respect to Thordeman and many others, we should be wary of one assumption, which is very prevalent in studies of the history of art and technology. That assumption is that any basic technological innovation necessarily arises in one location alone and disperses outwards from there. The creation of segmental armours like lamellar and scale is a technology which could easily have been invented in more than one location independently, with the flows of dispersal from any one locus of invention fluctuating over time.

The genesis of these armours may in fact lie in the late Stone Age. Across Europe and the Caucasus, graves have been found with assemblages of pieces of bone, horn or shell that have been pierced and somehow bound together as bodily adornments, sometimes in quite complex structures. It is notable that in some areas male bodies in particular had such structures encompassing their heads.[2] Otherwise, wide bands might enclose the throat or elbows, and there are larger masses that suggest skirts.[3] It is quite plausible to imagine that a man wearing such ornaments might well have found himself in a hunting incident or conflict situation which showed the potential protective value of such a bone or horn fabric and thereby led to the construction of a denser structure designed for that defensive purpose.

Another consideration to bear in mind in terms of technological development is that, just as it may not be singular and geographically contiguous, it also need not be chronologically continuous. A technology may die out and be revived, either anew or from artistic or physical survivals. This phenomenon is conspicuous in the cases of both these armours. For further discussion of this, see the introduction to the section on lamellar.

Sources for the armours

The sources for external small plate armours are fourfold:

Firstly, examples that have been preserved complete – or substantially so – in collections. These are confined to the modern era. Provided that the material has not been aggressively conserved, or modified to conform to contemporary tastes (as so much armour was in the nineteenth century), the information it provides can be taken at face value, and can shed light upon prior practice.

Secondly, archaeological finds. The condition, and hence information value, of this material can vary enormously. Much has been found as disarticulated fragments, and so these cannot in themselves be very informative. Even better-preserved examples have sometimes been misinterpreted by non-specialists dealing with the finds. A significant amount of the material in major collections was either excavated in what would now be considered an unacceptably unscientific manner, or else was acquired through the commercial antiquities market. The latter has long been prone to having the provenance details of artefacts embellished, or simply falsified, for a variety of reasons. Hence, one must sometimes be very sceptical of the information that accompanies some items.

Art works. This category forms the bulk of the source material, and is the most problematical. Ancient pictures and carvings are not photographs, nor are they technical renderings of any portion. They are works of contrivance, created for particular purposes: propagandistic, didactic, religious or entertaining. They are conditioned, at the least, by the social and ideological expectations of their sponsors and expected audiences, or by stylistic conventions, or both. The medium itself may constrain or determine the character of the depiction. Furthermore, artists varied in draughtsmanship skills, or in their familiarity with what they were employed to represent, or by the amount of effort expected of them in their execution, leading them sometimes to create sketchy or garbled renderings. Like films today, historical pictures are often contrived for visual clarity and drama, even when the result is physically impossible. Such an example can be seen in illustration 34, where the arm and sword of the central attacking horseman must take on an Escheresque dimensional distortion if he is to strike the man he is pursuing. Specific issues lie in the observation that occasionally artists used an expedient pattern which can look very much like scales in order to represent mail,[4] that horizontal banding which might be taken to be lamellar could be better interpreted as laminar or 'anime' armour,[5] and in the proper identification of the pattern that nineteenth-century scholars called 'banded mail'. As a result of all these considerations, no work of art can be taken entirely at face value. The study of historical armour generally is bedevilled by people determined to treat ancient and medieval pictures as if they were literally and completely accurate. One need only think of the trellised and broad-ring armours which nineteenth-century writers and illustrators made of the schematic depiction of mail in the Bayeaux Embroidery. Recent work encompassing external small plate armours, especially lamellar, has seen a considerable number of instances of this.[6] Another problem with pictorial sources is dating. Some art comes from archaeological contexts or with textual or other corroboration, which allows a degree of confidence. A great deal more, though, is only dated by the processes of art history analysis, which is purely impressionistic.

Given a certain artwork, an art historian may decide that it looks sufficiently like some other piece which has a commonly accepted date to propose that it must come from the same cultural milieu and period. If enough of his/her colleagues agree, then it becomes a 'fact'. The problem is that the date of the reference artwork was probably established by the very same process, or may date back to the origins of the discipline in the nineteenth century when intellectual deference allowed historians of sufficiently recognised stature to simply make a decree and have it accepted as fact. Such issues are especially rife in the Art History of the Byzantine Commonwealth.[7]

The final form of evidence is textual material. This is the most marginal form. Just as with the artists, it was rarely relevant to the goals of authors to be detailed and technically precise about the armour worn by the people about whom they were writing. The exception is, of course, military manuals, which can provide some extremely useful information, especially when correlated with art.

Reconstruction

As this is an intensely practical subject, practical experience and experimentation can provide valuable insights. In contemplating a picture, one may ask, 'Can it be built to look like that using techniques of the time?' and 'If it can be built to look so, is it functional?' The answer must be 'yes' to *both* questions before the reconstruction can be said to support an interpretation. Similarly, experience in making and using items can assist in seeing through the effects of damage or decay in archaeological items.[8] Yet, even acknowledging those parameters, we must bear in mind differences in outlook between ourselves and people in the past. Men in the past have in many situations been willing to put themselves in harm's way to a degree that can seem inconceivable today. The point of armour was more 'harm minimisation' than 'harm prevention' for most warriors. On the other hand, that consideration varies with the quality of armour. If a high-quality armour is reconstructed in a manner that has significant vulnerability, then it must be incorrect.

Such practical considerations cannot, however, stand alone, nor can they override other evidence and analysis. It can be perfectly possible to build a functional item on the basis of flawed evidence or interpretation. I cite the example of my own early theory about banded lamellar which led me to build a *klivanion* based upon Ian Heath's widely known over-simplified version of lamellar.[9] That *klivanion* was reasonably functional, and the inventiveness of humans means that it cannot be said that it is impossible that somebody, somewhere, made such an armour, yet today I can say that it is inconsistent with the great mass of data now available and should be rejected. Hence, reconstruction must be an adjunct to methodical and methodologically well-informed research.

In preparing this volume, new theories (and, indeed, some old ones) which were potentially contentious were routinely tested by the manu-facture of a sample.

Definitions of the forms

Past writers have struggled to come up with systematic definitions for these forms of armour.[10] Part of the problem is the confusion caused by the pictorial literalism I discussed above. Another unhelpful thing is the old-fashioned use of the term 'splint' in relation to such armour. That term, in my opinion, should be confined to armour made of long, narrow strips, normally used for limb protection.

I suggest a simple system, that external small plate armours are divided into three categories: lamellar, scale and a category for which there is no widespread term.[11] The overarching distinction between the first two is straightforward. When used in the *primary protection zone* (such as the torso of a human):

- scale armour overlaps *downward*, and is predominantly mounted on a continuous substrate, usually of textile or leather.[12]
- lamellar overlaps *upwards*, does not have a continuous substrate and its structure is created using some sort of cordage.

There are a few exceptions to these rules, but they are just that – exceptions, necessarily of limited scope.

The principal exception in the case of scale is the so-called 'semi-rigid scale' armour used in the early Roman imperial era, where the entire structure is made of scales fastened together with metal staples or ties, with no use of textiles or cordage as substrate or fastening. This only breaches the substrate aspect of the definition, for all surviving instances overlap downward, where a piece is sufficiently complete to infer its orientation. As discussed later (see page 53), there is a very limited set of pieces where scales overlap upward, but they are not used for the primary protection zone.

There are pictures suggesting inverted lamellar on the primary protection zone; however, it should be noted that those few pictures occur in a very limited period and cultural context. They are all in Byzantion or areas artistically derivative of it, and primarily clustered in the eleventh and twelfth centuries. They are also almost entirely in religious art, and are very often garbled in ways other than simply the inversion of the fabric of the armour. Their existence can be explained by the phenomenon discussed above – artists required to depict something with which they were not directly familiar and having to rely either on other pictures, which might themselves be defective, or on descriptions given to them.[13] There are even more cogent practical reasons for dismissing inverted lamellar in the primary protection zone. In the first instance, the 'amorphous' forms of hanging lamellar (see below for an explanation of these terms) do not hang in a stable manner when inverted. Depending upon where the suspension laces run from and to, the material will be prone to fall open to some degree. Once on the body they will be a little more stable, but the tendency to drop open would itself make the armour much harder and slower to put on, as each row would have to be arranged to hang flat. A still more pointed (pun intended!) counter-argument is explained in the following section on the protective functionality of the armours (see pages 16–20).

There are rare instances, however, where lamellar construction is employed overlapping downward for human (as opposed to equestrian) use (once again, confined to pictures from the Byzantine Commonwealth of the eleventh and twelfth centuries) but, as with scale armour, this application is only for limb pieces, and never in the primary protection zone.

Lamellar is itself divided into two micro-structural variants – 'solid-laced' and 'hanging'. In solid-laced lamellar, the vertical connection between the rows is close and tight, allowing little movement. This tends to be a characteristic of earlier forms. In hanging lamellar the rows are suspended on loose laces, allowing considerable vertical flexibility.

Hanging lamellar harnesses may themselves be divided into two macro-structural categories, 'amorphous' and 'structured'. (Solid-laced lamellar, and, indeed, scale armours, are inherently structured.) In amorphous hanging lamellar the only constraint governing the movement of rows relative to each other is the suspension laces. Hence, an amorphous lamellar is capable of telescoping more or less completely into itself, and when extended may undergo considerable lateral movement. Structured hanging lamellar has some sort of continuous binding at the ends of its rows to stabilise its fabric. This practice makes the armour much easier to use in donning and doffing, and more durable, although at the cost of making it harder to store and carry when not worn. The amorphous form was by far the more widespread and longest-lasting, being the dominant form in the East.

Terms for individual components of the armour will be used consistently and exclusively thus: *scale* = a plate used in scale armour; *lame* = a plate used in lamellar armour.

The third form of external small plate armour unnamed above is an unanticipated inclusion in this volume. Sometimes associated with the French term *broigne*, or more fully '*broigne* of plates', it is an armour with (usually rectilinear) plates fixed flat to a substrate garment without any sort of overlap. In modern hypothetical reconstructions they are commonly riveted to the base, although modern re-creators will also stitch on panels of (sometimes hardened) leather. Even though this type of armour is a staple of quasi- or pseudo-historical movies, there is virtually no evidence for it in the historical record. The origin of the idea of externally plated armour lies in the same habit of uninformed pictorial literalism of nineteenth-century antiquarians that produced the similar fanciful ideas of trellised and broad-ring[14] armour. There is a picture conjectured to be a *broigne* of plates in the *Stuttgart Psalter*, which shows a man whose chest is covered with a square lattice with dots in the centre of most compartments.[15] It has even exerted some appeal over recent archaeologists. Researchers investigating an early eleventh-century site at Lake Palandru in south-east France found a small group of iron plates about 50mm square with a single central rivet, and decided they came from such an armour. Their reconstruction shows plates spread very sparsely over a short jerkin, leaving great expanses of unprotected leather.[16] Facsimiles of this hypothesis made by re-enactors more sensibly place more plates closer together and sometimes even slightly overlapping, but this does nothing to alleviate one of the most basic problems with the theory. With a single central attachment, a plate might rotate, disrupting the coverage pattern, where there is one. Furthermore, as the garment flexes with the wearer's movements, any edge of the plate could peel away, allowing a weapon behind, if not to pierce the base garment and wearer, then possibly to tear the plate from the garment. Other hypothetical reconstructions of a *broigne* of plates employ the greater security of rivets in all corners, but all share the fundamental vulnerability of unprotected intervals between the plates. The supreme armament of Antiquity and the Middle Ages was the spear, a thrusting weapon. Any gaps between plates are obviously at risk. Nor are metal plates a foolproof defence: a committed thrust, especially at any angle to the surface, will skate and drop off an edge into the unprotected gap. For these practical reasons and for the lack of any persuasive evidence, externally plated armour must be rejected as fiction, except for the one Western example which has come to light, which can be found in the discussion of *culets* in the scale armour section (see page 53).

Materials

Surviving items of exterior small plate armours are, not surprisingly, overwhelmingly made of metal. Iron is predominant, with various copper alloys less common. Organic materials were certainly used in lieu of metal. The more limited survival of these is supplemented by literary references to horn, and more robust forms of leather such as ox hide. There is limited evidence to support the idea of more mundane types of leather being treated by processes such as boiling or wax impregnation in order to be used for these armours, although no one can say it was never done. Pragmatically, however, it is unlikely, for leather of that sort can be used to make large plate armours with much less effort.[17] One thing is quite clear – that leather is used for external small plate armour reconstructions in both re-enactments and films far more often than the evidence justifies.

The protective functionality of the armours

In combat that does not involve firearms, armour is confronted with four types of challenge: sharp impacts, blunt impacts, cuts and stabs. The following observations are based upon several decades of the author's involvement in re-enactment and military living history and in research-ing, practising and teaching Western historical combat forms.[18]

High-powered projectile impacts, whether sharp or blunt, from weapons such as ballistae, heavy crossbows and catapults, can be counted upon to overwhelm any man-portable armour system and so may be discounted from this discussion. Lighter projectile impacts, from arrows, quarrels, darts, javelins and sling stones, have the characteristic of being a momentary challenge to the resistance of the armour. Up to a point, small plate armours have an advantage in that a pointed projectile impact is more likely to penetrate something rigid, while the limited flexibility of small plate armours can have the effect of absorbing and dispersing much of the energy of the projectile. The author's tests have shown that this flexibility, combined with the multi-layering that is found in many versions of these armours, is outstandingly effective in resisting sharp projectile impacts.[19]

The primary protection zone is rarely a target for hand-held blunt impact weapons (i.e. maces) as they are much less likely to do debilitat-ing damage in that area. Once again, the limited flexibility of small plate armours tends to disperse the impact and make such attacks even less effective. Sharp impacts from hand weapons, such as axes, and back spikes on axes and hammers, are more problematical, for they have the potential to compromise the integrity of the armour as well as transmitting impact. The limited flexibility will have some impact-dispersal benefit, but ensuing damage will leave the wearer vulnerable to a further attack even if the armour does not fail catastrophically at the first assault.

Both scale and lamellar armours are highly effective against cuts. It might seem at first that the exposed lacing of lamellar might be a vulnerability, but in practice this is not so. The sheer quantity of laces that must be cut in order to compromise the integrity of the fabric is so great as to forestall it.

It is against stabs to the torso that the performance of different forms of exterior small plate armour vary most. In the less common situation of downward stabs, the imperviousness of scale armour hardly needs to be explained – the attacking blade will simply tend to skate off. In the case of lamellar in its normal overlapping-upward form, while the blade will lodge against the top of a row, the density of the structure prevents it from displacing plates enough to penetrate. Should the angle be so acute that the blade could slip down between the rows, it will have great difficulty in penetrating the body of the wearer. In practice, the majority of stabs, whether from spear or sword, are in the low alignment, and from there tend to angle upward to some degree. On scale armour, the effect will depend upon which construction variant is involved. With the most basic form, where the scales are attached only at the top and do not overlap laterally (*fig. 1*), a point skating upward can lift a single scale or a couple of scales and slide up underneath, thereby gaining access to the textile or leather substrate and penetrating it. To prevent this danger, various expedients were devised. A common approach was to punch holes near each edge a portion of the way down each scale (*fig. 2*) then to overlap the scales horizontally, allowing those holes to be used to fix all the scales in one row together, and sometimes to the backing as well. This meant that a thrust would have to lift almost the entire row in order to penetrate the garment, a rather more difficult thing to do, especially with the rows curving around the body. A further method was embodied in 'semi-rigid scale armour', used almost exclusively by the Romans of the early imperial era. In this type of armour, an additional pair of holes was made at the centre of the lower edge or point of each scale (*figs 3 and 4, and ill. 5*), and these were used to fasten the final loose facet of the scale down to that below.This style was essentially impervious to all thrusts, although its near rigidity limited its usefulness.Against (overlapping-upward) lamellar, once again the result is obvious – the point will skate upwards, at worst catching on the upper edge binding, if it exists. Should hanging lamellar be used inverted in the primary protection zone, it suffers a degree of vulnerability to upward-directed thrusts that is midway between that of the simplest form of scale armour and form with adjacent scales overlapped and bound together. A blade will skate up the lamellar plate, and then simultaneously lift the row above and push the impact row in and down. An amorphous hanging lamellar is extremely vulnerable to this phenomenon, and a structured hanging lamellar not much less so. Solid-laced lamellar is less acutely vulnerable, but still may suffer penetration through parting of the binding laces.Outside the primary protection zone, the precise dynamics of the threats are slightly different. The mobility of the arms means that cuts often arrive with less force, and makes them less of a target for thrusts, thereby reducing the lamellar/scale distinction noted above.Whereas thrusts to the torso tend to have a somewhat upward slant, thrusts to the thighs always have a downward angle. All the most forceful cuts are downward, and while they fall on the torso quite perpendicular to the surface, below the waist they may arrive at an acute angle to the surface, potentially offering a greater threat to lamellar in the usual overlapping-upward orientation.These considerations explain why lamellar torso armour was sometimes combined with mail, scale and inverted lamellar upper sleeves and skirts (*ill. 28*). This practice in fact predates the widespread use of lamellar in the Roman army, as there are representations of Roman armours with scale skirts as early as the first half of the first century of the Common Era (CE).[20]

Forms of the harness
An autonomous cuirass of exterior small plate armour may be constructed in four overall forms, which occur in both fabrics:

Chest and back only, with shoulder bands of leather or lames at right angles (may have separate skirts, possibly of the same material).
Chest and back only, continuous over the shoulders (may have separate sleeves and/or skirts, possibly of the same material).
Chest, back and legs continuous.
Chest and back with sleeves and legs continuous.

In addition, with lamellar, and the less flexible forms of scale armour, the portion that encircles the chest must open for access. Such an opening may be on one or both sides, or down the centre front. Front opening was rare, for it is a primary area of vulnerability. There is no evidence – whether archaeological, artistic, or by comparison to more recent surviving examples from further East – to suggest that cuirasses might open at the rear, and such a configuration is inherently very much less practical. Nevertheless, it cannot be said that a rear opening was never used.

Fastenings

Two methods of fastening can definitely be said to have been in use with both forms of exterior small plate armour. Lacing (that is, ties) was the most widespread practice across the broadest spread of time. Strap-and-buckle arrangements were introduced much later, with some of the earliest definite evidence being in the Niederstotzingen lamellar harness. Inspired by occurrences of mushroom stud connectors in early Roman use, the author has found an arrangement of straps and mushroom studs riveted into metal lamellae very effective (*ill. 37*), but this is a completely speculative arrangement which could be more prone to failure in high-stress combat situations.

Caveats

Finally, a note on what is wrong with this volume, and similar summary treatments. Ancient and medieval workmanship was nothing like what we may expect from our post-Industrial Revolution viewpoint. The scales and lames that survive are enormously variable in form, size and quality, even within a single contiguous armour piece, let alone within a deposit of material. Nor are they ever geometrically precise. Hence, all the diagrams in this book falsify what they represent by not showing the variation, and even more so by standardising and rectifying the form of any plate shown. Those who want a more authentic impression should read the archaeological reports.

Another caveat is that there is a tendency both with archaeologists and with secondary treatments, including this one, to assume that any given scale or lame represents a continuous fabric. Where one plate or a few plates have been found, this assumption is questionable, for specialised plates were often made to facilitate tailoring and finish edges and openings. For an example of this practice, contrast the edging plates on the Bourke scale helmet hanging (*fig. 11, type 1.11*) with those in the bulk of the piece (*fig. 11, type 1.10*).

Terminology

Historians and antiquarians of the nineteenth and early twentieth centuries studying historical and ethnographic arms and armour adopted foreign and historical terminology for less familiar items into English with great enthusiasm. Unfortunately, they did not employ an equivalent level of consistency nor, it often seems, a similar level of understanding about how the terms were used in their original context. More recent writers have not conspicuously remedied the situation.[21] Hence, I will generally avoid the use of such terminology, except in specific areas where my own training allows me a degree of confidence (i.e. Latin and Greek). With work in that early period being such a formative factor in modern museology, a great deal of such variable language is still embedded in museum records. A starting place for those who want to familiarise themselves with such antique terminology in order to facilitate searching is George Cameron Stone's *A Glossary of the Construction, Decoration and Use of Arms and Armour in All Countries and in All Times, Together With Some Closely Related Subjects.*

PART 1

SCALE ARMOUR

Scale armour has the widest use of these two armours by far. The components of scale armour vary enormously in size and shape, even within the same period and cultural context – and, indeed, sometimes even within the same harness. Its variability in terms of construction, however, was much less extensive than that of lamellar. At the end of the nineteenth century, while studying the material found at Carnuntum in Austria, and presumed to be Roman,[22] Von Groller created a typology of scales seemingly based upon factors of overall size and shape, and the size, shape and placement of the holes.[23] Von Groller's typology is, on one hand, unnecessarily complex, comprising nine types on the basis of distinctions which he does not precisely define. On the other hand, it fails to accommodate types of scale not employed within the cultural milieu of the deposits he examined. A simpler, universal typology can be defined based upon the construction method, which determines how a given scale fabric functions in use.

Typology

Scale armours may be classified by the method of fixing, and hence their flexibility and protectiveness, thus:

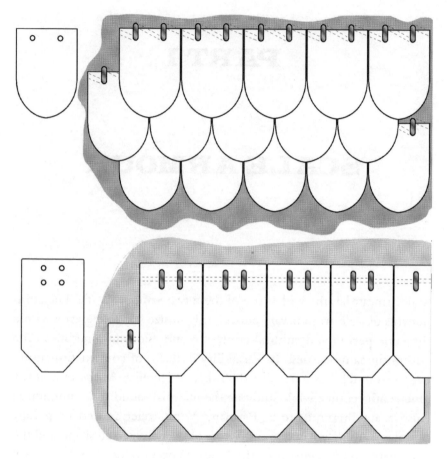

Above
Fig. 1 The most common basic forms of scale assembly. Above, Type 1. Below, Type 2. The binding may also cross the edge on Type 2.

Opposite, top
Fig. 2 A sophisticated Type 4 assembly from Carpow, Scotland. E: edge binding. P: padding cord

Opposite, centre
Fig. 3 A semi-flexible Type 5 construction from Carnuntum.

Opposite, bottom
Fig. 4 A semi-flexible Type 5 construction from Carnuntum.

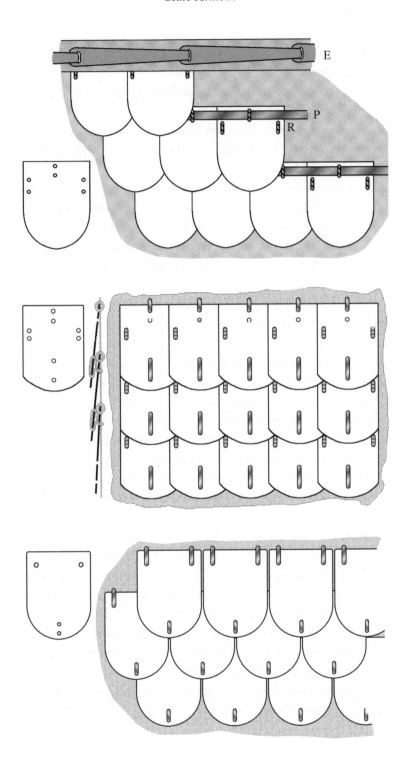

Type 1 – secured only near the concealed edge through a single row of holes.

Type 2 – secured only near the concealed edge through a double row of holes.

Type 3 – secured near the concealed edge by either of the above methods, but with an additional fastening through a single hole partway down.

Type 4 – secured near the concealed edge by either method, but with additional ties through pairs of holes partway along each edge.

Type 5 – secured near the concealed edge by either of the first two methods, and at the opposite point through one or two holes, and often on all four cardinal points ('semi-rigid scale').

The collection of examples of scales from archaeology in Figure 1 is organised according to this typology. Types 1 and 2 are ubiquitous and occur across the entire duration of this study. The rare type 3 occurs almost exclusively in medieval Russia. A question must remain over the distribution of type 4. To date, all surviving examples are believed to be Late Antique and from Roman, or closely related, contexts. However, in addition to the caveat in note 22, the great majority of the medieval source material for the use of scale armour is pictorial and offers no evidence of the method of construction, except in suggesting that it is not type 5. Type 5 is the other form which appears from all present evidence to be culturally and temporally localised, used from the second to fourth centuries in the Roman empire. Even in the Roman realm, the semi-rigid scale is clearly a minority form.

Figure 1 shows that the size and shape of the plate are unrelated to its typology according to construction. This constructional typology is more significant because it relates inversely to the flexibility of the fabric created with the scales, and consequently relates directly to the protectiveness of the armour. Type 1 armours are most flexible, but least protective, because they are most prone to the possibility of plates being lifted by an attacking weapon, especially by a thrust, allowing penetration through the substrate. The more extensive binding of type 2 means that the base material must be moved more in order for the plate to lift, and is therefore more resistant, while type 3 takes this premise further. Type 4 scales are commonly overlapped laterally and fastened together, thus requiring most of a row to be lifted for access to the interior to be gained. At the other extreme, the variety of type 5 that is made without a backing and the plates fastened together with metal staples (type 5b) is the most protective, but a virtually rigid material (5). The degree of rigidity determines how any given scale fabric may be used.

Other pragmatic observations on the modes of construction of the various types are thus: A lateral overlap on type 1 and type 2 scales with holes near the centre confers little advantage. Where type 2 scales have holes close to the edges, lateral overlap can be used with common binding to gain some stability advantage. Type 3 scales are said to have been riveted at their lower fastening.[24] While that is likely to be true for examples such as those shown in Figure 1, type 3.5 (*fig. 5, top*), for the others with a hole close to the edge this additional fastening is more likely to be textile like the top attachment, and protected by the overlap of the adjacent plate (*fig. 5, bottom*). Type 5 is commonly known as 'semi-rigid'; however, with the type assembled from plates fastened together with wire ties, there is very little 'semi' about it! The expression would be more fitting for the backed variety where the lower fastening can be arranged to allow some flexibility (*figs 3, 4*). In deference to established terminology, here I use the term 'semi-flexible' for type 5a.

The flexibility of scale armour, and the potential for tailoring in the substrate, allowed it to be used for an extremely wide range of applications, from modest discrete pieces such as helmet hangings or gorgets, to complete garments covering the whole body. One area upon which scale was hardly ever used for functional armour was the head. This may seem at first to be a questionable comment, given that scaled helmets do appear in art, and there are even surviving examples, but it is an area in which the flexibility of scale is precisely *not* what is needed. The surviving scaled helms are solely among the '*karacena*' armours popular in Poland in the seventeenth century. They were, however, purely parade armours (see below). In addition to sporadic Roman depiction (*ill. 1*), scaled helmets occur from time to time in Greek vase painting. Several factors indicate that those represent decoration rather than construction.

The helms in question are perfectly ordinary Corinthian styles in overall form, and the scaling covers only the crown, leaving the lower portions plain, representing solid metal, or very occasionally patterned in a different manner. Furthermore, there are parallel examples where the crowns of such helmets are patterned in ways that do not even approximate hypothetical construction methods.[25] They must consequently be taken to be purely applied decoration.

Construction

There are three methods of construction employed in making scale armours. They are: stitching or tying with textile or leather, riveting, and tying with wire. The first is by far the most common, the last the least used. Riveting is confined to late examples that are either for parade use, or are peripheral pieces that will be subject to fewer attacks or stresses. The reason for this is durability and repairability. First, riveting is not suitable for a textile base garment because the very process of making a hole or driving the rivet through damages the structure of a textile, making failure more likely. When scales attached to the substrate by organic material fail, the failure is usually in the binding material, leaving the foundation material less damaged and hence the armour more repairable. Failure in riveted scale armour invariably involves significant damage to the base material. Wire ties were not used for anything other than binding metal scales together in type 4 armours where the lateral fastening does not involve the substrate, and in type 5b armours.[26]

The Bronze Age to the Hellenistic Era

The earliest evidence for scale armour appears in Egypt in the second millennium BCE. A considerable number of bronze scales have been found in various locations from as early as the start of the fourteenth century. Correspondingly, a scene from the tomb of Ken-Amun at Thebes shows scale armour in golden colour. Plates found in the palace

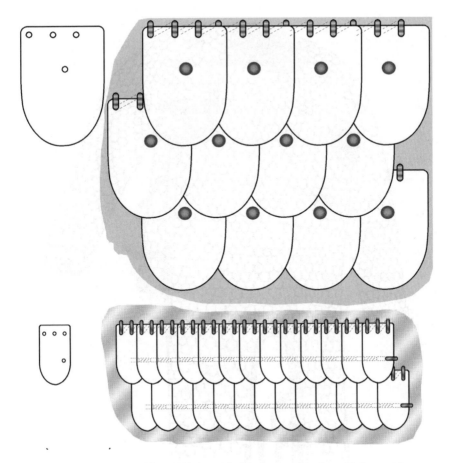

Fig. 5 Type 3 scale assemblies. Above, with supplementary rivet. Below, with supplementary textile binding.

of Amenhotep III (1410–1372 BCE) at Malqata, Western Thebes, had residues of a linen backing, while a reference in the *Annals* of Thutmose III (1525–1516 BCE) implies leather substrate.[27] Early Egyptian armour scales are uniformly of type 1 and rounded. A dominant characteristic is they are squat, often wider than they are deep (*fig. 11, 1.1–3*).

Skythian tombs in the region of northern Ukraine dated to the early fifth century BCE yielded extensive scale armours in various configurations. Bodies were found clad from neck to ankle in scales. One example has been reconstructed as a hip-length, long-sleeved shirt, accompanied

Fig. 6 Reconstruction of the Skythian scale harness from Alexandrovka, end of the sixth century BCE.

by full-length leggings similar to chaps.[28] Another seems to have been a single garment with body, sleeves and legs all in one (*fig. 6*).[29] The latter armour, especially, looks forward to the entirely scale-clad Roxolani horsemen of Trajan's Column. Unfortunately, the records of these finds were lost, and much of the material itself suffered a similar fate. It may be inferred, though, that these armours must have been predominantly, if not entirely, composed of type 1 or type 2 scales, for no other would allow the flexibility that such all-encompassing armours require.

The ever popular paintings of warriors produced in many contexts in ancient Greece frequently show corselets of the classic form – a short breast and back with shoulder straps fastened by ties at the front and having a skirt of *pteruges* below. The scale coverage shown on these corselets can be quite variable. Some have them only on the body itself, leaving the shoulder straps and *pteruges* plain. Others have scaled body and straps, with plain *pteruges* only, while others are scaled in all portions. Overwhelmingly, the scales are the organic scale shape, and small, appearing to be about 40mm wide and of similar overall length. One Greek vase found in Italy shows a curious hybrid. The upper part of the chest down to the armpits shows scales like those just described, while the lower portion has large square scales very much like those shown on Etruscan artworks (see below). The question arises whether this was a product tailored to the Etruscan market, or whether the larger scales were used in Greece as well as in Italy. A *kylix* by the Sosias Painter (*ill. 2*) showing Akhillês bandaging Patroklos shows outstanding detail – the side view of Akhillês confirms that the form behind the shoulder is the same as seen on other Greek and Etruscan armours, and the unlaced shoulder strap of Patroklos's corselet reveals the profile of the chest-piece. The lack of any surface detail on the scales lends further support to the conclusion that these, too, were made of type 1 or 2 scales. Furthermore, the fact that centuries of Classical collecting and archaeology have yielded scarcely any traces of such armour suggests that they were rarely, if ever, made of metal, but rather of the less durable materials – leather, horn or bone.

The Greek colonisation movement planted so many cities in southern Italy during the eighth to sixth centuries BCE that the Romans referred to it as 'Magna Graecia' or 'Great Greece'. Such extensive contact resulted in a great deal of trade, and the sharing of military technology between the Greeks and the Etruscans. Although the prolific finds of armour consist overwhelmingly of muscled cuirasses in bronze, Etruscan artworks and Greek-style works found in Italy show scaled corselets, but generally with detail quite distinct from Greece itself. The corselets are of familiar Classical construction, yet the scales shown on the artworks in Etruria are large, rectilinear and decorated (*ill. 3*). These scales are depicted as being about 80–100mm long by 60mm wide, and are most likely to be made of embossed or incised leather.

Herodotos makes several references to scale armour, although not in connection with the Greeks. He states that the Persian and Median soldiers of Xerxes' army invading Greece wore 'intricate sleeved garments … covered in iron scales like fish to the sight'.[30] This description suggests a rather more sophisticated and protective style of armour than that of the Greeks, having something in common with the contemporary Skythian examples previously discussed. In connection with the Battle of Plataia (479 BCE), Herodotos tells us that the scale armour of the Persian cavalry commander who fell there, Masistios, was gilded.[31]

Late Antiquity

Rome: Republic and early empire
The Romans of the early imperial era were past masters of scale armour. Their enthusiasm for it seemed to know no bounds. It is represented in countless works of art, and to confirm that this was not merely creative contrivance, physical remains of scale have been found across the length and breadth of the empire. The general Latin term for a scale corselet was *lorica squamata*. A special expression, *lorica plumata* ('feathered') was reserved for armour made with scales having a rib down the centre.[32] Precisely when they added scale armour to their repertoire is open to debate. The Royal Ontario Museum has a very impressive *lorica squamata* said to have been found at Lake Trasimene in 1863.[33] Unfortunately, this armour was an early twentieth-century acquisition from the commer-

cial antiquities market, where provenance details were (and are) often very unreliable, and it is recognised as a composite assemblage incorporating some modern elements. Even if the location were accurate, there would be no basis for associating it with the battle which took place at Lake Trasimene in 218 BCE. Nevertheless, the majority of the material of the armour is accepted as being ancient, and so it is worth noting that the approximately 600–650 scales are bronze, of type 1 with two holes, mostly rounded, and 25–40mm wide by 41–57mm long, except for those which have been placed along the hem in the (modern) reconstruction which are distinctly longer (80–85mm).

A great deal of more reliably dated art and archaeology does, however, show that scale armour was already well established in Roman use in many variants by the turn of the Common Era (CE). It is significant to note that, contrary to Greek and Etruscan precedents, and contrary to the preference Romans themselves maintained for centuries for mail shirts and for having semi-detached shoulder straps drawn forward and fastened on the chest, from the earliest depictions Roman scale armours show integral vests running unbroken up the chest and over the shoulders. This suggests that Roman scale use was influenced from the outset by 'barbarian' practice, rather than from within the Classical world. This influence may have come from the north-east, from the Skythians, or from Egypt, or perhaps from both directions at once.

The Campidoglio Monument (*ill. 4*) erected by Emperor Domitian (81–96 CE) is an important early example. It shows a *lorica plumata* in the form of a sleeveless Classical *thôrax* of the form known from elite muscled cuirasses, with ornate *pteruges* below. This may represent a triumphal parade armour, yet its form defines a modular practice in Roman scale armour which will persist for more than 1,200 years. In the context of it possibly being a parade armour, the originally gilded bone scales from Pompeii may be the remnants of just such a piece.[34]

A funereal stele in the Verona Museum shows another interesting permutation. The man commemorated wears a shirt that fully encloses his shoulders and has a hint of sleeves, and terminates on the thigh in a skirt composed of a double layer of scale-covered tabs which are themselves scale-shaped.[35]

Roman archaeology has yielded scales of all types except type 3. Type 4 seems to predominate across the late republic and empire. The type 5 secured with wire survives in the largest pieces, due to its intrinsic durability, but does not come into use in the second century and seems not to survive beyond the fourth.[36] Across that span of time it does appear across the breadth of the empire. A particularly interesting example of type 5b is an assemblage found at Carlisle in England. It comprises three rows of scales wired together, each scale being somewhat teardrop-shaped and the elements in each row graduated in size so that the entire piece forms an arc. The scales of the bottom row have no holes at their ends, and so we know that was as far as the piece was intended to go (*fig. 11, type 5.3 & 4 and type 4.4*). It may originally have been a gorget. Similar tailoring can be seen in a much larger piece found in Palestine (*ill. 5*). The best evidence for types other than type 5 suggests that heavy cloth was the most common base for Roman scale armours, with finished pieces sometimes being edged with leather (*ill. 6; fig. 2*). Type 4 scales were assembled in two different ways. One construction binds overlapping scales together with wire ties without involving the base fabric. The other binds them to the substrate as well as to each other with a textile binding. The latter method produces a substantially less flexible, but somewhat less vulnerable, armour.

More extensive encounters with peoples to the north-east through the second and third centuries evidently broadened the Romans' scale armour repertoire. The booty shown on the reliefs on the base of Trajan's Column includes finely rendered scale shirts providing greater coverage than had been seen on earlier Roman sources, including elbow-length and wrist-length sleeves, and helms with scaled neck guards (*ill. 7*). Pictorial material confirms the continuity of scale armour in Roman use to the fall of the western provinces.[37]

In addition to type 5b, the Romans indulged in another unique application of scale. It is a hybrid of scales and mail (*lorica hamata squamataque*, sometimes erroneously called *lorica plumata*).[38] Type 1 scales have the top bent backward at ninety degrees to allow them to be linked into the fabric of a mail shirt. Very little of this form of armour has been found, just four deposits, from Vize in Thrace dated to the early first century at one extreme of geography and time to Newstead in Scotland, dated late second century, at the other. The specimens are in both iron and copper alloy. The very nearly complete corselet from Vize follows the common form of an early imperial mail shirt in the Classical arrangement of being mounted on a leather base with semi-detached straps folding forward over the shoulders fastened with bronze hooks. Its scales are unusual, as they are tapered but squared off at the bottom with rounded corners. It has a vertical strip of plain mail down the right side. This will have been left to facilitate donning and doffing, for the combined mail and scale fabric would not have the degree of horizontal expansion of normal mail. The suggestion has been made that *lorica hamata squamataque* was parade armour, although that is a contentious idea.[39] It is certainly not at all clear that this construction would have had any protective advantage, given the lightness of the materials required to make it feasible, and flexibility of the scale to mail linkage. This armour may have been no more than an example of Roman conspicuous consumption.

The Near East

The empires of the region encompassed by modern Iran are in many ways the great untold story of the ancient world. The historical record from the end of the Greek invasions to the advent of Islam is rather patchy and often inaccessible in the English-speaking world. There is certainly no reason to assume that scale armour would have fallen out of use in the 500 years following the Persians' defeat by the Greeks in the Persian Wars, yet at the same time there is very little hard evidence to shed light on the situation. There were no developments which could begin to replace it, even with contacts with Mesopotamia bringing lamellar more to their attention. Moving into the Common Era, evidence becomes more prolific. From 238 BCE to 224 CE Iran and adjacent regions were included in the Parthian empire under the Arsacid dynasty. After a period of decline in the late second and early third centuries CE, Persians from eastern Iran overthrew the Arsacids, ushering in the Sassanian era, which lasted until 642. The transition period of warfare generated a slew of large-scale stone-carved depictions of crucial moments in the conflict, some of which are well enough preserved to offer good evidence for armour. Mail clearly predominates in these sources, but scale does appear. Noteworthy is the battle scene of Hormuzd II (302–309) at Naqsh-i-Rustam which shows Hormuzd and his standard-bearer clad in scale armour.[40] Elsewhere, when mail is the primary body armour, scaled collars or helmet hangings can be seen. Type 2 and type 5a scales, along with lames and perforated metal plates of a perhaps more specialised function, were excavated at Old Nisa dating from the first or second century CE.[41] Early in the Sassanian era the Persians moved against the Roman empire, destroying the Mesopotamian city of Dura-Europos in 256. That siege left a great deal of military equipment behind, which remained well preserved in the dry conditions. A large amount of scale is among those remains. Some is regarded as being Roman, but an intact scale horse armour has been attributed to the attackers. This barding is a single piece designed to cover the horse from shoulder to rump, with a panel around the chest, and an opening in the centre to allow for the saddle. It leaves the horse's neck undefended. The scales are bronze, type 4, as are the great majority of those from Dura-Europos (*ill. 6*). They are quite large, in the vicinity of 50mm square, and very bluntly rounded. The likelihood is that even though the evidence from the whole of the Sassanian period shows that mail was the preferred armour for man, and one or other exterior small plate armour for horse, were the dominant practices, it is likely that some use of scale armour for men persisted, perhaps for infantry soldiers.

The Middle Ages

The Roman empire after the fall of the western provinces (Byzantion)
Traumatic as the fall of the western provinces of the Roman empire was for Western Europe, in the East, it was mostly business as usual. The evidence is clear that continuity prevailed militarily, albeit a continuity which adapted and evolved to accommodate social, economic and technological changes, as had always been the case. The crucial technological

development of this era was the advent of the stirrup, which the Roman army adopted in the late sixth century. The adoption of the stirrup fundamentally changed the balance of effectiveness in the forces. Prior to this, cavalry was the secondary arm, useful primarily for scouting, harassing and skirmishing. Riding into fully fledged combat without stirrups could be done, but required a high level of skill. With stirrups, men with lesser equestrian skills could fight effectively from horseback, taking the fight directly to the enemy. This made greater use of armour desirable, while the stirrups made greater use of armour more possible. This change is represented in the *Stratêgikon*, attributed to Emperor Maurice and completed around 602. The literature of the previous century had added a new term, *zava* (ζάβα), to the ancient expression for a corselet, *thôrax*, and to *lorica/lôrikion*, a general term for armour with a slight tendency to mean mail. The sources use *zava* inconsistently, and while modern scholars generally lean toward it being a mail shirt, the possibility of a padded garment is acknowledged.[42] Several references in the sources indicate that those two options do not exhaust the possibilities. *Perì Stratêgías*, a manual from the sixth century, includes a sequence for efficient arming of a soldier.[43] It clearly dissociates the armour for the thighs from that of the chest. No such separation is needed or appropriate for mail or padding, indicating that the author has some more solid armour in mind. It is true that that division need not be made with scale armour either, but that is a subject I shall return to. Further confirmation can be found in the observation that on two occasions the *Stratêgikon* mentions techniques for reducing the chance that the enemy will recognise the equipment at a distance.[44] The wording used suggests that the armour in question would be bright or shining. Padded armour could be faced by a colourful cloth, but its difference from clothing would not be readily discernible from afar. Iron mail does not shine. Even if not fire-black, it is no more than dull, dark grey, or rusticated. Only armour made from metal plates could be bright or shining. It is unclear whether Romans had begun to adopt lamellar at this time, but we can confidently assume the earlier Roman mania for scale armour had not vanished entirely.[45] The *Stratêgikon* describes the ideal *zava* as falling to the ankle and accompanied by a separate hood.[46] Some commentators

have been inclined to doubt the length of that armour,[47] but it is perfectly feasible if it refers to mail, and, as we have seen with the Skythian
graves, ankle-length scale shirts had been used long before. A Coptic
fragment in the Rylands Library corroborates this by showing St Menas
riding in scaled armour to the ankle with elbow-length sleeves and what
appears to be the skirt of a hood (with no discernible patterning and so
perhaps fabric) above it around his shoulders.[48]

The period from the end of the first half of the seventh century to the
late ninth century is often called the 'Dark Age of Byzantion'. A succes-
sion of external attacks which repeatedly threatened the city itself were
followed by a violent religious dispute about whether it was legitimate to
make illustrations of holy persons drastically curtailed all forms of cultural
production. The economic harm done by these events must have depleted
military resources as well, yet once large-scale literary and artistic production resumes from the tenth century we see that the arms and armour
paradigms of Late Antiquity to the Middle Ages transition period remain
largely unchanged. In perpetuating the *Stratêgikon's* recommendation for
ankle-length armour, the *Taktika* of Emperor Leo from around the start of
the tenth century gives us more information, saying that if they cannot be
made of mail, they may be constructed of horn or ox hide.[49] These materials are not only contrasted with mail, but also with lamellar, and thus
must be used as scales. Secular pictures of warriors were popular alongside
the warrior saints through the middle Byzantine era (886–1204). Both
classes of soldier can be seen clad in scale armour, and all the previous
approaches to making scale armour still existed – the singular integral
corselet covering just the chest and back (sometimes with semi-detached
scale sleeves), a *thôrax* accompanied by a scale skirt, and longer one-piece
shirts with sleeves. In addition, there are a few instances of scale sleeves
and skirts attached to a lamellar *klivania* (*ill. 28*). Most of the pictures show
scales of very familiar form. Some, however, show details which might at
first sight be taken to be fanciful or distorted but for archaeological finds.
A few pictures in the eleventh and twelfth centuries show large rectilinear
scales comparable to some found in Russia (*ill. 10*).[50]

Evidence for the late Byzantine period (1204–1453) is very sparse and
problematic. Literary sources shed very little light on military equip-

ment. Secular art is virtually non-existent, while the depictions of warrior saints are far more stylised than they were before. This is especially true of representations of armour, which are very garbled. Pictures that are closest to plausibility have patterning that suggests scale armours, both the more common sort and the rectilinear Russian type.[51]

Al-Islamiyya in the early centuries

The righteous zeal that impelled the first Muslims out of the deserts of Arabia did not blind them to the recognition that the societies they took over were much more culturally sophisticated than the one from which they had come. Even before the advent of Islam, border-raiding must have brought them into contact with the use of external small plate armours by adjacent neighbours, the Romans to the west and the Sassanians to the north, yet there is little evidence for large-scale use of those armours permeating across the border. In capturing great swathes of territory from them, they also took control of the industrial base that supplied such equipment, thereby allowing them to adopt such armour if they chose. Unfortunately, establishing the degree to which they chose to do so is very difficult. The erratically applied Islamic prohibition on depicting animate beings reduces the amount of visual art there might otherwise have been in the early centuries to virtually nothing, while the potential of written material is very inadequately exploited. Most of what has been published in English on arms and armour in early Islam is quite unreliable, largely due to the fact that the authors were not able to read sources in the original languages.[52] Alas, I do not have the linguistic skill to remedy that lacuna, but hope to clarify the situation a little with a more practical eye.

Accessible literary material tends to suggest that the Arabs who had become the new ruling elite did not choose to adopt either form of exterior small plate armour extensively, preferring to retain the use of mail that had been familiar to them in Arabia. Thus, the use of those armours in their armies must have remained with the contingents drawn from the various peoples over whom they now ruled – Christians of

various communities, Persians, Armenians and others. The Christian-
occupied areas had been part of the Roman empire, and, as is discussed
further in Part 2 (see pages 98–9), at the time of the Muslim conquest,
lamellar does not seem to have made any notable inroads into Roman
military practice but, of course, scale armour had been a great Roman
staple. Later sources do suggest a degree of continuity as well as new
trends imported from the great patriarchal capital to which Eastern
Christians looked: Constantinople.

Eastern Europe in the Age of Migrations

The diverse tribes whose westward migrations had precipitated the
collapse of the western provinces of the Roman empire undoubtedly
carried their own arms and armour practices with them. As we have
seen, the regions from which they originated, or at least passed through,
had traditions of exterior small plate armours going back to the earliest times, and so the practices were carried outward in their migration.
The most copious evidence for this is in lamellar (see the next section),
but scale is by no means absent. Contrary to Thordeman's theory, the
armour from Kunszentmárton in Hungary is, in fact, a scale harness,
not lamellar.[53] More recent finds from Germany to the Crimea have
added to the tally of scales associated with the Avars. The unusual shape
of these plates, and the fact that most of the other finds from this area
and period are lamellar, makes the failure to recognise them as scale
somewhat understandable, but in the case of Kunszentmárton, at least,
the archaeological report is very explicit.[54] A curious feature of this
armour, according to modern aesthetics, if nothing else, is that it was
made up with the shaped edge of the scale concealed, thereby giving a
simple rectilinear chequerboard appearance to an onlooker. The excavators determined that the approximately 220 plates were stitched with
thread to a base of heavy fabric, creating a sleeveless, hip-length corselet. Other unusually shaped scales from this period and cultural milieu
have been found at Dilingen and Kirchheim/Reis in Germany, and
Kertch in the Crimea.[55] All are type 4 scales. Scales from Kirchheim

(*fig. 11, type 4, 12*) and Kertch (*fig. 11, type 4, 14*) must have exhibited the same simple, rectilinear appearance when made up in any form. While the scales from Dilingen (*fig. 11, type 4, 13*) and another from Kertch (*fig. 11, type 4, 15*) might have been assembled with the shaped edge concealed like the Kunszentmárton, alternative assemblies offer different and thought-provoking possibilities. Depending upon precisely how they were assembled, their finished faces may have looked quite like lamellar, and yet without the full range of visible lace or edging details that a comparable lamellar system would exhibit (*figs 7, 8 and 9*). This may well go some way towards explaining the otherwise anomalous and seemingly stylised patterning on some depictions of armour through the Middle Ages in Western Europe and elsewhere.

Western Europe

In the centuries following the migration period, Carolingian art showed very well rendered depictions of scale armour. Whether they are representations of real objects or not, the forms of armour shown are manifestly derived from a Roman tradition, rather than that of the migratory tribes discussed above. The question of the realism of those pictures continues to be debated. Thus far, archaeological investigations of north-western Europe in the early Middle Ages have yielded no finds of pieces of scale to corroborate the paintings, but that is largely true of all Carolingian armour. The literary sources for the area are also irritatingly vague. Coupland remarkably concluded after his survey of the evidence that scale armour was not in use, and that its depiction was due to imitation of Byzantion, while claiming that the most common antiquarian armour shown in Carolingian art, the Classical muscled cuirass with *pteruges*, was actually in use![56] That was, however, with the reservation that the evidence 'does not allow categorical conclusions about Carolingian body armour to be drawn'. In discussing other pieces of military equipment, he does recognise that the art can be corroborated against archaeological finds, thereby confirming their realism, in those details, even when accompanied by armour he dismisses as based upon

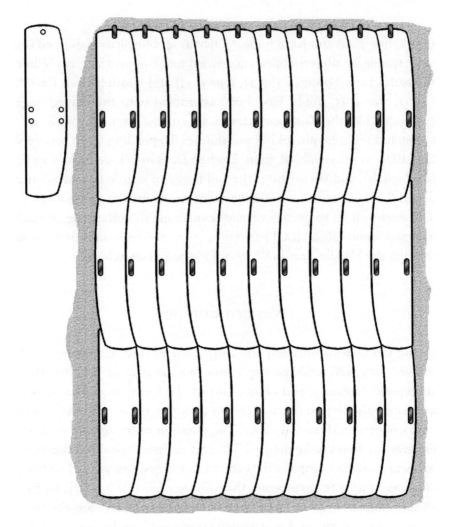

Fig. 7 Hypothetical reconstruction of the scale from Dilingen, Germany. The rows might equally be oriented with the scales all in the same direction of course.

Byzantine artistic precedents. More recently, Bachrach avoided any consideration of what Carolingian soldiers employed as protection at all.[57]

The *Stuttgart Psalter* of around 830 offers the most precise and plausible array of pictures of scale armour. Its armours run the gamut of the most functional forms – hip-length corselets,[58] thigh-length infantry shirts with elbow-length sleeves,[59] to knee-length cavalry shirts with

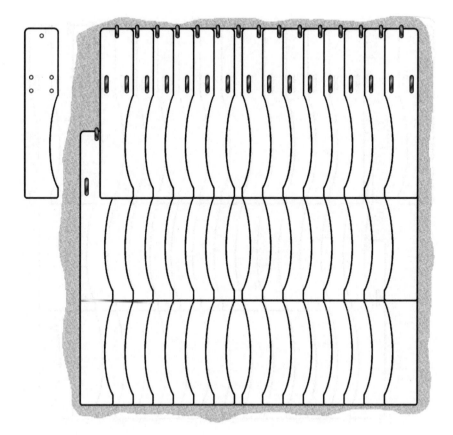

Fig. 8 A hypothetical reconstruction of one of the scales from Kertch, Ukraine.

sleeves to the wrist (*ill. 8*).[60] Other permutations are especially informative. The hip-length corselets show the curved and bordered lower edge profile that is so familiar from Byzantine armours. What is more, many of the longer armours, which have not been included in the tally above, show a division between the chest and the skirt which follows the same lower curve, sometimes rendered in a leathery brown, contrasting with the blue-grey iron of the armour (*ill. 9*).[61] This feature of apparently continuous scale armours divided by a curved hip-line is very familiar in Byzantine and Byzantine-influenced sources, as we have seen.[62] The significance of the feature had not been fully clear despite the mention in military manuals of separate chest and thigh armour, because scale *thôrax*

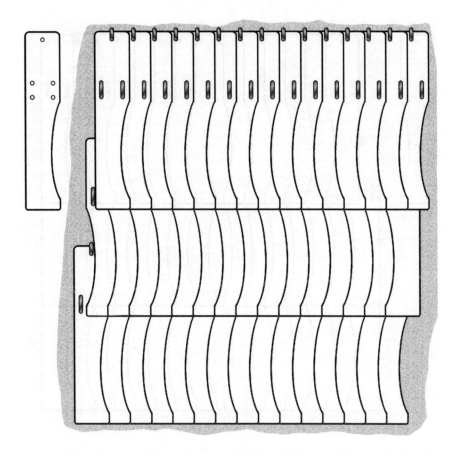

Fig. 9 An alternative hypothetical reconstruction of one of the scales from Kertch, Ukraine.

and scale skirt are never shown separated in any surviving art of the Byzantine Commonwealth. Several pictures in the *Stuttgart Psalter*, however, explain it completely. The first appears very early in the volume, a scene showing two men in scale skirts without any other armour.[63] Later, a scatter of discarded military equipment includes a short corselet and separate skirt lying apart on the ground.[64] Elsewhere, there are two men who have corselets of different construction, accompanied by a scale skirt.[65] Finally, just before the end of the *Psalter*, a picture of Goliath further confirms the observation – his sword belt disappears up under the breast armour, just as it would if fastened around his waist after a skirt but before the upper corselet was put on.[66] A literary reference places the seal on the matter. The Monk of St Gall, describing Charlemagne at Pavia, talks about him wearing separate thigh armour: 'The thighs, which with most men are uncovered that they may the more easily ride on horseback, were in his case clad with plates of iron.'[67] The practice of using a corselet and separate skirt of some different construction is well documented in the Roman world from the republican era to the tenth century, if not beyond.[68] The same practice was employed by the Avars in their lamellar armour shortly before the Carolingian period. The artists of the *Stuttgart Psalter* clearly understood how this armour functioned and, as noted above, seem not to have had a Byzantine *artistic* precedent for the separation of chest and skirt. Thus, the conclusion is inescapable that scale armour *was* in use among the Carolingian Franks. One picture in the *Stuttgart Psalter* adds a pleasing cosmetic detail. It shows a shirt with a row of brass scales at the collar, yellow contrasting with the blue iron of the majority of the shirt.[69]

The Caucasus

The nations of the Caucasus, most notably Armenia and Georgia, were open to influences from the East as well as the West. As Orthodox Christian peoples, they naturally looked to Constantinople first, and Armenia, at least, was a vassal state of Byzantion for long periods of time. Unfortunately, their production of literature and art that would be useful to us is less extensive, and also often derivative of Constantinople. The last factor makes handling the sources that do exist a delicate challenge. Nevertheless, with such strong traditions of exterior small segment armour in all their adjacent nations, we can be sure that it was in use.

The best source for Armenia is the Church of the Holy Cross at Aght'amar, built in 915–19. Among the façade carvings are three warrior saints, Theodore, Sergios and George. All are equipped with short-sleeved scale corselets which extend down to the upper thigh. The scales are shown as having blunt, rounded ends, a similar shape to figure 1.4.1,

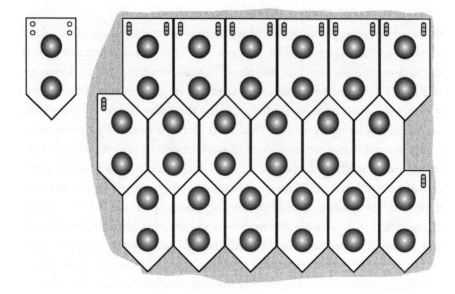

Fig. 10 A possible distinctively Georgian scale style.

although their large size probably owes more to the convenience of the carver than technical accuracy.

Manuscript illumination flourished in the later thirteenth century in Armenia, and provides some excellent views. A scene in one volume in the Freer Gallery of Art shows an extensive scale shirt accompanied by a separate hood with scale protection around the neck and throat.[70]

Georgia is much better supplied with pictorial sources, with pictures of warrior saints being produced extensively in the tenth to twelfth centuries and its own manuscript tradition for centuries from then on. The great majority of the early icons are executed in embossed metal and vary enormously in the quality of representation and plausibility. As far as they can be trusted, these icons seem to suggest that the Georgians had a distinctive style of scale. Its form is a narrow, pointed plate with one or two embossed dimples (*fig. 10*).[71] One can compare these icons with surviving scales from Tiffliskaya Stanitsa in Russia which are an identical shape, although are much smaller and with only a single dimple (*fig. 11, type 1 & 7*). The corselets shown in these pictures are the expected functional form – hip-length with short sleeves.

Russia and Scandinavia

The Russians made notable use of scale armour through the medieval period. They also employed a wider range of shapes than other nations, including some unique forms. Noteworthy among type 1 scales are those which have the unusual characteristics of being wider than their depth, and having a double, or even triple, curved edge at the bottom (*fig. 11, type 1, 5 & 6*). This form is so distinctive that it seems reasonable to hypothesise that the instance found in Germany got there either as a result of a Russian incursion, or with a Russian mercenary (*fig. 11, type 1, 4*). The small, polygonal scale with a boss from Tiffliskaya Stanitsa (*fig. 11, type 1, 7*) bears some resemblance to the Georgian icons discussed above, which are, of course, from a similar cultural milieu. The Rus would certainly make a scale of very simple, familiar style, as can be seen from a find from Tenginskaya (*fig. 11, type 2, 7*), yet even with type 2 scales they might adopt an idiosyncratic approach. A corselet in the State Historical Museum, Moscow, attributed to the thirteenth or fourteenth century, has curious square plates fixed only through two lines of three holes in one corner, seeming to imply an unsecured horizontal overlap (*fig. 11, type 1, 9*).[72] Evidently the maker did not consider lateral angled thrusts which would readily lift a scale to be an unacceptable threat. A twelfth-century soapstone icon, also in the State Historical Museum, shows St George in an armour which elucidates the form in a familiar direction. His upper body is protected by a hip-length corselet with short sleeves and an edging sweeping down over the belly, and below that by skirts which guard his thighs almost to the knee. The whole panoply is made of large square plates conspicuously overlapping horizontally in one direction (*ill. 10*).[73] Each of the scales is shown as having a defined margin on the exposed edges. The medieval Russian preference for scales presenting a rectilinear face to the world may have originated in the Avar presence in the Crimea in Late Antiquity. Russia's unique contribution to scale armour is type 3, which is almost unattested anywhere else. Type 3 employs a secondary stabilisation attachment part of the way down the scale, but unlike type 4 which uses that as well, type 3 only has a single secondary attachment. In most cases this is evidently meant to be a textile binding, just like the primary ones, which is to be protected by a lateral overlap (*fig. 11, type 3, 1–4; fig. 5, lower*), but there is one example where a rivet does seem to be implied (*fig. 11, type 3, 5; fig. 5, upper*). Once again, the archaeology shows that the Russians were perfectly capable of making a 'standard' form of type 4 scale (*fig. 11, type 4, 7*), but still preferred rectilinear shapes (*fig. 11, type 4, 16–17*). Among the small deposit of armour plates recovered from the stockade of the Swedish royal capital of Birka, destroyed around 970, there were two types of scale, along with the three types of lamellar plate. The quantity of pieces, and the disparity in the types, indicate that this was neither a single corselet, nor a stock of complete armours. Rather, it is most likely to have been a scrap-metal collection awaiting recycling. One of the scales is a typical type 3 (*fig. 11, type 4, 5*). The other is a rectangular type 4 (*fig. 11, type 4, 17*). Both are of characteristically Russian style, and were probably souvenirs brought back to Sweden by a seafaring Viking, rather than anything made or used locally. (See the more extensive discussion of the Norse evidence in Part 2 on pages 93–7.)

The Near East

As noted previously, the Arab Muslims who came to rule the Near East did not embrace exterior small plate armours. Yet it is clear that scale armour, at least, remained embedded in the martial repertoire of the subject populations of the Levant. As the Middle Ages continued, this was reinforced by influences from various directions. Christian communities, including the Crusaders once they were established, looked naturally to the local Christian great power in Constantinople, which is known to have provided a certain amount of economic and military aid.[74] Art produced in the Levant shows various instances of scale armour as supplementary pieces (sleeves and skirts) combined with lamellar, as well as scale armour alone (*ill. 28*).[75] Magnificent pictures of scale armour from the Crusader States are found on two icons, which are now in the Monastery of St Catherine on Mount Sinai. One shows St Sergios with a female donor and the other saints Sergios and Bakkhos. All are shown in the guise of 'Turkopoules', mixed-race medium cavalry, armoured with finely rendered shirts of fine scales to mid-thigh with elbow-length sleeves.[76] Unfortunately, levantine archaeology of the Crusades era has not yet offered any physical traces to elucidate fine details such as what scale types were in use.[77]

Scale armour had a role in the armour suite of Iran in Late Antiquity, but it is impossible to establish securely how, or even whether, its use continued through the first five centuries of the Islamic period. Whatever the situation, in the late tenth century a new tide of conquerors with their attendant cultural influences swept into the region from the north-east – the Seljuk Turks. By their own images of themselves as much as anything else, the Seljuks seem to have worn little armour. The few images of armoured men that exist show exterior small plate armour, in the form of short jackets with short sleeves, but the media and style of the majority of the pictures do not allow any firm judgement of which type(s) of exterior small plate armour were intended.[78] A manuscript produced in the twelfth century by a people beyond Iran who were by then newly subject to the Seljuks' rule, the Rômiosi of Anatolia,[79] is more detailed, showing that they wore scale armour, as well as lamellar. One picture shows a scale shirt with sleeves all the way to the wrist.[80]

The next incursion into the region came a little over two centuries later in the form of the Golden Hoard. The Mongols are much like the Avars in that, while their use of lamellar is well known, their employment of scale armour is under-appreciated. The reason for this is the same as with the Avars. It is that the shapes of the plates they used were often not of a familiar or organic scale shape but very similar to the shapes of lames. Scales have been found in Mongol archaeological sites,[81] but the best evidence is to be found in the many fine illuminated manuscripts produced in Iran in the fourteenth century. Scales of familiar shape can be seen, perhaps indicating native continuity, and made into long front-opening coats with elbow-length sleeves (*ill. 35, centre, and ill. 36, far left*). Elsewhere, we find long scales very much like some surviving Avar examples (*ill. 35, far right; compare fig. 7*). Residual Mongol influences on Iran faded through the later fourteenth and fifteenth centuries and the Iranian cultural outlook opened again a little more in a westerly direction. In terms of military equipment, this led to the adoption of composite mail and plate and the so-called 'mirror' armours, which resulted in the use of scale, as well as lamellar, falling out of use.

Eastern Europe in the later Middle Ages

Cultural boundaries are never impervious, and it may be the proximity of Russia that made a contribution to the continued use of scale armour in Eastern Europe in the later Middle Ages. A German manuscript from the early fourteenth century shows a crossbowman whose panoply harks back to Byzantine precedents – a short scale shirt with a separate skirt of larger scales.[82] A little later and further east, the *Wenceslas Bible*, made for King Wenceslas I of Bohemia between 1390 and 1400, shows scales used as skirts attached to bascinet helmets.[83] Another Bohemian manuscript of the fifteenth century depicts more extensive applications – scaled skirts below breastplates, and in one case accompanied by a scaled gorget.[84] These scale examples accompany plate armour of otherwise familiar metropolitan European style and undoubtedly represent the last use of scale armour west of Russia until the nineteenth century.

Southern Europe in the later Middle Ages

'Mediterranean' literally means 'Mid-Earth', and that sea has always been more of a highway than a barrier. As a result of this, the lands of the European littoral remained realms of cultural fusion. In the Iberian Peninsula, of course, the cultural intersection was direct, as Muslims occupied it from 711. Their rule was only rolled back gradually from the eleventh century, and that process did not involve large-scale expulsions of the Muslim and Muslim-descended population until the very late stages. Even prior to the Moorish conquest, the peninsula had had a long history of exterior small plate armour. Scale armour had already been in use prior to the Roman takeover, and was doubtless reinforced by the Roman passion for scale, while lamellar had been carried in by the migrating tribes at the time of the fall of the western Roman provinces.

As previously observed, mail had been the armour of choice for pre- and early Islamic Arabs, and insofar as the post-Roman inhabitants of North Africa had sophisticated military equipment, it was doubtless the same for them. Finding themselves ruling the more settled and affluent territories that would become Spain and Portugal, it was understandable that they would take up the customs of more solid protection that they found. Certainly, by the middle of the Reconquista period when there are a much greater quantity of good sources, scale is very much in evidence. The most impressive sources for this era are a group of gorgeous illuminated manuscripts made for King Alfonso X in the last quarter of the thirteenth century. The quality of depiction in all of them is of exceptional realism, and offers many insights into the cultural fusion that Alfonso is regarded as being especially active in fostering. One in particular, the *Cantigas de Santa Maria*, contains many battle scenes.[85] The Moorish forces are generally shown as being less heavily armoured than the Christians, although that may to some degree reflect the common Arab and Moorish practice of comprehensively covering armour like mail with textiles. Scale armour tends to be depicted as more used by the Moors, but it is by no means confined to them. In Christian use it is clearly characterised as a poorer infantry armour, with the cavalry clad in the all-enveloping mail that was by then universal across Europe. The scale shirts in the *Cantigas* are consistently shown as thigh-length with short sleeves. The scales are quite large (probably owing more to artistic convenience than accuracy), most commonly round and marked in a way that suggests that they are fluted or somewhat domed. In shape and the latter profile they can be correlated against the surviving shirt in the Alava Municipal Museum, whose date span encompasses the period (the twelfth to fourteenth centuries).[86] The Alava shirt is made of type 1 iron scales around 30mm square mounted upon fabric. It is sleeveless, and has an opening down the left side. The colours applied to the scale shirts on the *Cantigas* are highly variable, although never within a single shirt. There are shades which could suggest scales made of all the usual materials – iron, bronze, horn and bone – yet there are also tinctures which would never occur naturally in any of those materials, such as red, so questions remain. Bone and horn are amenable to dying (and, of course, painting), although why that would be done on a second-rate scale armour is debatable. Red may indicate leather, which comes out of some tanning processes that colour, as well as being able to be dyed. In terms of literary material, it seems that the Spaniards had evolved a consistent terminological distinction, using *loriga* for a mail shirt, and *lorigón* for a scale shirt, and having a term for a hood attached to a *lorigón*.[87] The sources indicate that the use of scale armour continued in Spain into the fourteenth century, although the contexts in which it is found in (religious) art may suggest that with its Moorish associations and with the Reconquista accelerating, it may have been falling out of favour for ideological reasons as much as a result of the development of larger plate armour.[88]

Another realm of significant cultural fusion was Sicily. The island had had a diverse history – Hellenic, Roman, Muslim and then Norman from the late eleventh century. The Norman policy of rule was less cultural coalescence than cultural co-option. The Siculo-Norman kings deliberately set out to take the mantle of Christian imperial legitimacy from Constantinople through artistic patronage. As a result, Sicilian art of the late eleventh and twelfth centuries must be approached with caution as evidence for real objects. Depictions of exterior small plate armour are a notable issue. Across the sources, lamellar is always represented in such a garbled form that we can be confident that Sicilian artists never saw it.[89] The situation with scale is less clear, if only because it is much harder to get it wrong. (You can be sure they saw fish!) It is very likely that the paradigm visible in Spain also applied in Sicily. The elite warriors of the ruling class wore the mail they were used to on the mainland, while some poorer infantry, especially when drawn from the subject populations, wore scale armour.

Moving on to the mainland, an outstanding twelfth-century relief depicting David defeating Goliath is to be found on a pediment of the Church of St Gilles du Gard in Southern France.[90] The fallen Goliath is clad in a beautifully rendered shirt of fluted scales falling to mid-thigh and with elbow-length sleeves. It would be hard to believe that the stone carver would have created such a precise representation without being familiar with a real item.

The late Middle Ages saw a trend for political and economic power to be increasingly concentrated in the north and west of Europe, and for steadily greater cultural integration, particularly in military technology. Hence, it is reasonable to infer that the trend towards the disappearance of scale armour in favour of mail and larger plate armour would also have overtaken southern Europe from the later thirteenth century.

North-western Europe in the later Middle Ages and Renaissance

It seems that the use of scale in north-western Europe did not much outlast the ninth century as the use of mail became ubiquitous. The reason for that was probably to do with the production process. A mail shirt can be completed by a single artisan. A scale armour requires two sets of skills – a metalworker to make the plates, and a textile worker to create the foundation garment and stitch the scales on. Scales do make a brief resurgence when, from the later thirteenth century, knights decided that a higher level of protection was needed than merely mail. While the primary line of evolution was for surcoats to be reinforced within, culminating in the coat of plates of the fourteenth century, there are a few instances of surcoats reinforced with very large scales on the outside from shoulder to the bottom of the rib cage, sometimes with a narrow fringe of similar scales hanging from the shoulders.[91] It seems likely that such large scales would have been made of hardened leather, for the larger a metal plate is, the more susceptible it is to deformation, and the weight of iron scales of that size would stress the substrate much more in flexion.

The next significant appearance of scale armour in northern Europe began in the seventeenth century in Poland. A great many scale armours were made and many survive. These armours range from scanty breast-pieces to complete outfits which may include scaled helmets, gauntlets and leggings (*ill. 11*). It is commonly the case that the corselet only covers the front, being held at the back by crossing leather straps. These outfits are invariably made of type 1 scales riveted to a leather base, which is often covered in an opulent and/or highly decorated cloth. The ensemble may include extravagant shoulder plates and chest bosses, often in the form of lion heads. The reason for the opulence of these armours, and fact that so many survived despite being made in an inherently fragile manner (see the comments on riveting in the Introduction), is that they were purely parade equipment. There is no evidence of any continuous tradition of use of scale armour in Poland, nor any military reason why there should be, given how well integrated the Poles were into the pan-European technology of sophisticated and effective plate armour. Although they are known as 'saracenic' armours (*karacena*), their creation was prompted by the ideology of 'Sarmatism', which claimed that the Poles were descended from the ancient Sarmatians, who fought against the Romans in the second century. The helms often do have a stylised turban fixed around the brow band, making a modest 'saracen' reference, but the primary inspiration for them came from Roman sculptures such as Trajan's Column (*ill. 7*) and others. An example like the Ludovisi Sarcophagus may have been a particular influence, in that it shows a scaled helmet (*ill. 1*).

Classicising inspiration may also lie behind an outbreak of more functional scale and pseudo-scale armour on the cusp of the Modern era. In the seventeenth century, with gunnery becoming a more potent force on the battlefield and use of pike blocks having rendered heavily armoured cavalry almost irrelevant, many horsemen in England abandoned iron in favour of buff leather. In addition to coats, these lighter horsemen wore gauntlets with long cuffs of buff leather or vambraces (forearm guards), some with gauntlets attached (*ill. 13*).[92] Most often these were constructed with the outer layer composed of bands of leather cut and arranged to resemble scale armour, but a few were genuinely of true scale construction. As these forearm defences required no flexibility, and because the leather would have tended to feather out in an awkward and unsightly way if unsecured, they were commonly constructed in the manner of type 5 with a fastening at the points, whether they were scales or scalloped bands. A noteworthy exception is one Royal Armouries Museum example, which replicates type 3 scales with a central fastening. This fashion for scaled buff leather items does not seem to have lasted past the seventeenth century.

Southern Europe in the Renaissance

The development of plate armour from the fourteenth century rapidly eroded the serious military utility of scale armour, and ultimately caused its disappearance even in those places where it persisted longest, Italy and Spain. Following close behind it, as the end of the sixteenth century approached the evolution of increasingly effective firearms similarly sounded the impending death-knell of plate armour. The combination of increasing social wealth, improvements in industrial production, and perhaps a sense of that approaching irrelevancy, produced a phenomenon in which life imitated art – a great indulgence of the use of extremely ornate parade armours. As the very ideology of the Renaissance was the claim that the cultural sophistication of Classical civilisation had been reborn, it is hardly surprising that many parade armours produced in Italy were inspired by the many surviving Roman monuments. Breastplates styled after opulent imperial muscled cuirasses had pride of place in this trend, of course, but scaled armour also saw a revival. Often the scaled appearance was simply *repoussée*,[93] but one fabricated example is now in the Hermitage Museum in St Petersburg. The basis is a perfectly ordinary late sixteenth-century iron breastplate, but its entire surface has been covered with bone scales riveted on, accompanied by grotesque masks and other classicising motifs.[94]

Yet the use of the scale revival in the late sixteenth and seventeenth centuries was not wholly cosmetic. One area of the body cannot be covered with metal plate if the wearer is to sit astride a horse – the buttocks. With the backplate of an armour ending at the waist, this can leave a significant area of vulnerability even when the man is seated, if the cantle of the saddle was not so high, as was often the case in this period. To reduce the risk, some Italian armours of the early seventeenth century were fitted with a rear skirt, or *culet*, covered in iron scales (*ill. 12*). The predominant form of such skirts is to have type 1 scales riveted on inverted; that is, overlapping upward.[95] There is a sound practical reason for this arrangement. In battle, one of the most dangerous situations for a cavalryman is to find himself bogged down in the midst of hostile infantry. Plate armour is largely impervious to cutting attacks, so thrusts were the primary offensive mode, hoping to find some small gap in the armour. Any thrust delivered by a foot soldier against a horseman is, of course, going to be directed upward. A *culet* with scales overlapping downward would be very vulnerable to such an attack, but with the scales overlapping upward, it becomes impervious as an upward thrust simply skates off. The *culets* in the Wallace Collection and the Royal Armouries Museum further affirm the strategy because in every case the top row of plates is flanged to overlap the back plate on the outside, thus ensuring that there is nothing to arrest the upward trajectory of the thrusting weapon.

One surviving but incomplete set of *culet* plates in the Royal Armouries collection is the sole known representative of the third class of external small plate armour. The plates are slightly lozenge-shaped, and in four graduated sizes creating an arc encompassing approximately a third of a circle and 130mm wide. The plates have two rivets at the top, and three at the bottom and evidently were not intended to overlap in any direction, but to lie flat edge-to-edge on the leather base. The close riveting on the bottom edge would resist the penetration of a point, although this variety of armour could never be as impervious as true scale. Armour with plates attached flush to the outside of a garment is a staple of the modern film industry, and there are indeed pictures which might appear to show armour of that sort. There is, however, no archaeological evidence to support that interpretation, and good practical reason to doubt it. An armour made that way would be extremely vulnerable to thrusts as the point of a weapon would skate across the surface of a metal plate to lodge in the interval between plates, and perhaps penetrate. This risk was evidently not deemed to be a great issue in this marginal and rarely challenged application.

The Modern era

It has been suggested that the disappearance of scale armour from the martial repertoire of Spain perhaps did not take place before Hispanic colonialism took it to the New World. In the first quarter of the twentieth century, a large number of scales (120) was found near the town of Aztec in New Mexico by a local banker. For almost half a century this discovery was merely a local curiosity known to few, but in the mid-1960s it was rediscovered and became more widely known. The site was then unsystematically scoured by curiosity-seekers. This process added greatly to the number of scales found, but resulted in them dispersing into many hands. It has been estimated that the total was around 500, sufficient to make a substantial shirt.[96] One group of these scales was donated to the San Juan County Museum Association in 1995, and more recently some others entered the Metropolitan Museum.[97] The scales are type 1 with two rivets. Their form is extremely regular and the classic 'heater shield' shape – rectilinear at the top and curving to a point from about halfway down, 26mm wide and 40mm long. The three straight sides have a distinct lip. In section they are slightly domed with a shallow ridge down the centre. Metallurgical analysis indicates that the iron was smelted using a bloomery process. The only remnants of the base garment were textile fibres retained under the rivets. Various theories have been inconclusively canvassed for the origins of this armour, while a Metropolitan Museum publication offers the explanation that this armour may have been an antiquated family hand-me-down made in the later fifteenth or early sixteenth century before being brought to America by a poor soldier/settler.[98] This suggestion is, however, negated by an earlier assemblage found in New Mexico, and by surviving material from elsewhere.

Around 1870, Captain John Gregory Bourke came into possession of a panoply consisting of a breastplate and back plate and a helm with a scaled skirt which is said to have been found enclosing human remains. As with the Metropolitan Museum group, Bourke hypothesised that the armour had come from Spain with a sixteenth-century soldier.[99] The cuirass, whose form and workmanship would probably have established the date of the set firmly, are, unfortunately, said to have been stolen during Bourke's lifetime. The remaining pieces of the John Gregory Bourke armour are now in the collection of the Nebraska State Historical Society. The construction of the helmet skirt (*ill. 14*) is of very high quality, and a unique technique. The scales that make up the body of the skirt are utterly identical to those in the Metropolitan Museum

– precisely the same shield shape, the same size, and with the same lip around the three sides of the top (*fig. 11, type 1.10*). There are also more or less rectangular scales creating a straight edge along the bottom (*fig. 11, type 1.11*). Like the Aztec scales, the Bourke scales have been determined to be bloomery iron, a process which ceased to be used in the early nineteenth century.[100] The scales are not attached directly to the base fabric of the skirt. Rather, they are fixed with two rivets to a cotton tape, which was then sewn to the base (*ill. 15*). Such a method of construction is entirely unprecedented in premodern history. It would be highly unsuitable for bodily use in hand-to-hand combat with pointed weapons, for it is even more flexible than type 1 scales fastened directly to the base garment and thus even more vulnerable, with plates lifting to allow penetration underneath. Another curious and modern feature of the skirt is that remnants of leather straps are attached with screws, rather than rivets. Further dating information can be deduced from the helmet to which the scaled skirt was attached. It is a shallow, more or less hemispherical iron bowl made in a single piece with rolled edges and slightly slanted, slightly pointed peak, also with rolled edges. A very strange feature is a large, precisely circular, opening in the crown, which is not due to damage, and which shows no sign of having had any attachment removed. The helm bears no close resemblance to European military headgear of the late Renaissance. The resemblance between the Aztec scales and those of the Bourke armour is so precise that it cannot be accidental.

Another artefact in the Metropolitan Museum sheds further light on the matter. It is a scaled bib-apron designed to be an early bulletproof vest, donated to the museum by the Ordinance Department of the US Army, having been made in France and used at the siege of Paris in 1870.[101] The scales of the bib are quite unlike the New Mexico group, being simple flat rectangles, but they are attached in the same distinctive way – fixed with two rivets to a tape which is then sewn to the base garment.[102] This group of correlations, between the form and material of the two groups of New Mexico scales, and between the modern construction of the Bourke helmet hanging and the Paris bullet-proof vest, is sufficient to draw the conclusion that they are all nineteenth-century

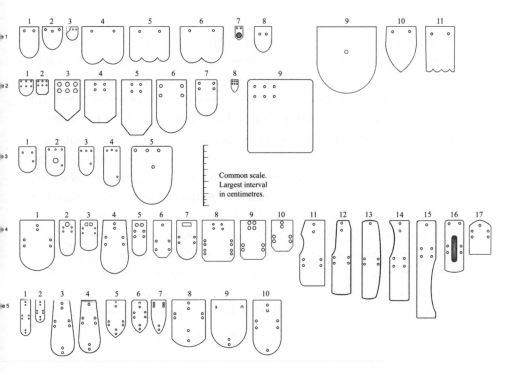

Fig. 11 A sampling of scales from archaeological finds. See page 118 for location and period details.

artefacts. The nineteenth century was probably the greatest period for scale manufacture since the early imperial period of the Roman empire. The ubiquitous passion for antiquarian romanticism, particularly focusing on the Middle Ages, led to the production of enormous amounts of new armour, as well as renewed attention being paid to original armour. Such armour was used for pageants like the famous Eglinton Tournament, and fraternal society rituals, as well as in the theatre. Theatrical productions of Shakespeare and the like, and historical operatic extravaganzas like Wagner's *Ring Cycle*, were staged with meticulous attention to historical, or, at least, quasi-historical, detail. The arms and armour created for these various uses were very often made to standards that could well have been militarily functional (*ill. 16*). The Paris scaled vest was certainly made for serious military use, and there is enough reason to think that the New Mexico armours were intended so as well.

Through the majority of the nineteenth century, that region of North America remained an area of endemic conflict, with colonisation, native resistance and European powers vying for control. Even in the context of formal warfare between states, the large-scale use of firearms had still not completely eradicated the use of body armour, even in the infantry, let alone among the often more traditional cavalry. In the less formal, long-distance cavalry operations that characterised the south-western area of North America, firearms were much less dominant. Prior to the use of brass cartridges, which were first employed in the mid-1840s but were not universal until the 1870s, it was virtually impossible to reload personal firearms while on the move on horseback. Hence, when battle was joined, after an initial brief volley which exhausted the revolvers and carbines to hand, any combat continued with hand weapons – lances, swords and so on. Thus, the usefulness of body armour continued through much of the century, probably explaining the presence of the Bourke panoply and the Aztec scale shirt.

PART 2

LAMELLAR ARMOUR

Lamellar is by far the most variable of the external small plate armours. The extreme diversity of lamellar constructions is potent evidence that this armour was not a singular invention which dispersed from one point of origin. There are forms of lamellar which are so radically different in their structure that they could not have evolved from a common ancestor, let alone one from the other. Furthermore, there are elementary forms which reappear over such vast gulfs of space and time, thus suggesting a direct connection is not credible. It must be concluded, therefore, that while some patterns of transmission and evolution can be observed in the historical record, lamellar armour was a technology invented and reinvented anew time and again.

That extreme diversity of structures also means it is impossible to create a typology of lamellar forms in the way that is possible for scale armour. Lamellar structures can be categorised thus:

- Integral – where the initial assembly of the rows is done entirely by tying lames to each other without any backing.
- Edged – where an initial stage of assembly involves wrapping the edges of the rows with strips of leather.
- Backed – where a strip of flexible material (usually leather) extends along the back of a row of lames to support or stabilise it. The backing

substance is sometimes wrapped over the edge of the plates onto the outside of the armour, but need not be so.

- Banded – when the backing extends beyond the top edges of the plates to create a plain division between the rows.
- Solid-laced – where the rows are bound firmly together with little movement in any direction.
- Hanging – where the rows are bound loosely, allowing some degree of movement, mostly in a vertical direction. A hanging lamellar may be sub-categorised as:

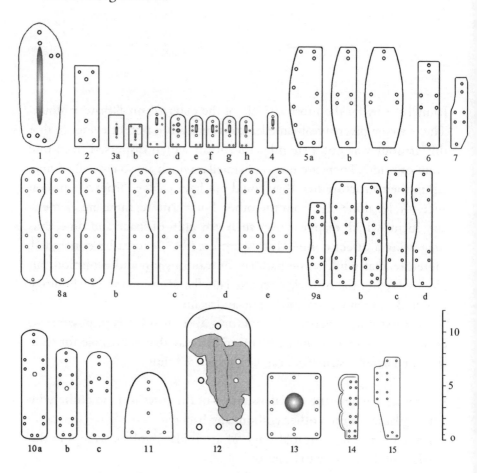

Fig. 12 Lames from archaeological finds. See page 118 for location and period details.

- Amorphous – when the only connection between the rows is the suspension laces, allowing lateral as well as vertical movement.
- Structured – when the ends of the rows have been stabilised in some manner, such as a continuous binding.

The Bronze Age

Like scale armour, the oldest evidence for lamellar is found in Egypt in the second millennium before the Common Era. A group of bronze plates of a very organic leaf shape embossed with a ridge down the centre was found in the ruins of the Palace of Pharaoh Amenhotep III at Thebes and dated to 1390–1353 BCE (*fig. 12.1*).[103] Fragments of linen cloth found adhering to the back of some of the plates have led people to assume they were scales to be mounted on a continuous base fabric in a manner somehow similar to one semi-flexible type 5 form (*fig. 4*).[104] Such an interpretation is not viable, however, for that method of assembly leaves the transverse pair of holes near the point unable to be used, as they overlie the solid metal of a lower plate. All the plates of the group are punched consistently, including that pair of holes, and it is unlikely that they would be made so for no reason. Thordeman noted two plates from Lisht in Egypt of a similar period which are of significantly different shapes, but show the same characteristic of having diagonally opposed pairs of transverse holes.[105] Plates found in 2006 in the so-called 'Palace of Ajax' on the Greek island of Salamis which are stamped with the cartouche of the Egyptian Pharaoh Ramses II (1303–1213 BCE) also have this arrangement of holes. A more viable reconstruction is that all these plates were assembled as a backed hanging lamellar (*fig. 13*). The Malqata lames would thus be stitched to a band (apparently of linen in this case) through the pair of longitudinal holes at the point and the single central hole at the round end, with a lateral overlap covering the upper transverse pair of holes. The suspension laces then run (entirely concealed) between them and the lower transverse holes of the plate above. If the suspension laces are direct, succeeding rows hang offset to each other by half a plate. By crossing the suspension lace as in the diagram, the rows naturally hang with the lames aligned, and have a little more lateral stability. The range of plates found suggests that this armour was well established in the New Kingdom of Pharaonic Egypt. It is remarkable that this earliest surviving lamellar from so long ago should be such a sophisticated construction. It is still more remarkable that, being so sophisticated, it did not survive and spread further. It remains a unique structure. It will be observed that the type of lamellar that becomes most dominant and persistent in the Ancient Near East is a very different and less sophisticated form.

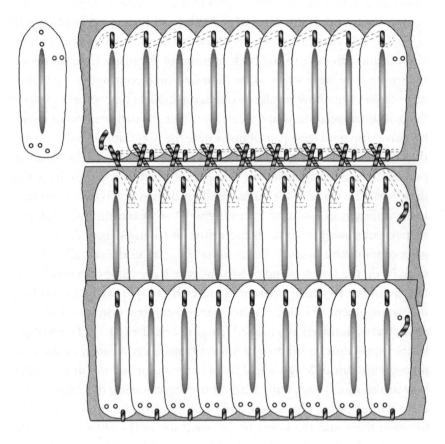

Fig. 13 Reconstruction of plates from the Palace of Amenhotep III, Egypt *c.* 1390–1353 BCE.

Next, we move on some 400 years to Persia. A rectangular copper alloy plate from approximately the ninth century BCE from Hasanlu has a much simpler regular punching arrangement (*fig. 12.2*).[106] If this plate represents a complete fabric, there are a number of ways it might be reconstructed. The lames might simply be overlapped laterally and have their edges wrapped together, yet that would leave the holes on the centre line unused. Furthermore, with metal-to-metal contact at the lacing point, flexion would wear through the binding rapidly. An alternative is that the central holes were used to tie the plates to a backing strip as a first step. That might be done with the lames overlapping laterally as just described, or merely adjacent. In the former case it would serve to ease the row lacing stage and make the armour more durable, both by virtue of the backing padding the lacing point, and by preventing a plate from falling away should there be substantial damage to the row lacing. The plate binding lace lies beside the edge of the upper plate and is thus protected from damage (*fig. 14*). The multiple row binding laces proposed in the reconstruction will reduce the possibility of localised damage running on, and might also be tied off behind. In the case of lames mounted adjacent with no lateral overlap, it would significantly reduce the amount of material required and hence the weight, by about one-third, but at the cost of making the row binding much more sparse and the fabric concomitantly less durable.

The Assyrian reliefs that are preserved in the British Museum and elsewhere show a great array of armour, much of which appears to be varieties of external small plate fabric. The reliefs are dated from the mid-ninth century to the late seventh century BCE. These artefacts have been discussed extensively in the literature, but no definite conclusions have been drawn.[107] The reason is understandable. Most lack the details which would elucidate the structure. The most modest form of harness is the ubiquitous hip-length and sleeveless model,[108] while the other extreme represents corselets down to the calf with sophisticated shoulder arrangements incorporating short sleeves onto the biceps.[109] In contrast to the dominant paradigms of later eras, the long armours only occur on infantry, and cavalry wear the least extensive armour. One variety of these armours, long suits just mentioned, shows fabric that is remarkably like that shown

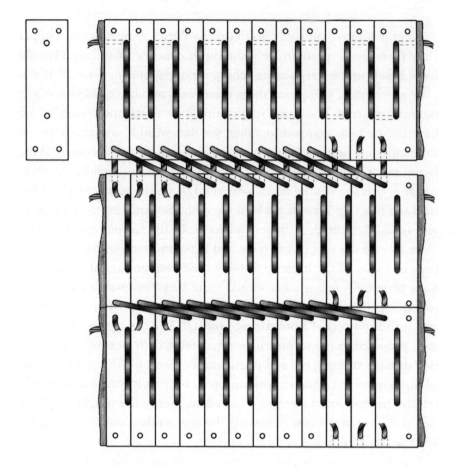

Fig. 14 Reconstruction of the lamellar from Hasanlu, Iran, *c.* ninth century BCE.

in middle Byzantine pictures of lamellar – plates with semicircular tops which do not appear to overlap horizontally, and rows separated by a plain band. What is conspicuously absent, however, is any representation of laces or other fastenings on the outside. That same blankness is a problem with the cavalrymen's jackets, again banded, but patterned with plates depicted as rounded on both ends (*ill. 17*). As Thordeman recognised, some of the reliefs do show assemblies that can be more readily analysed.[110] That armour is made of narrow rectangular lames bound end to end with braided thonging (*ill. 18; fig. 15*). There is as yet no archaeological material

1 Detail from
the Ludovisi
Sarcophagos,
Roman, mid–third
century CE.

2 Detail of a
Greek *kylix*
showing Akhillês
and Patroklos,
turn of the fifth
century BCE.

3 Etruscan figurine, fourth
century BCE (British Museum)

4 The Campidoglio
monument erected
by Emperor
Domitian, 81–96 CE

5 Remains of a shirt of Type 5b (semi-rigid) scale, Hecht Museum, Haifa, Israel, third century CE.

6 Fragment of scale armour from Dura-Europos showing textile backing and laced leather edging, mid-third century CE. (Yale University Art Gallery, Dura-Europos Collection)

7 Detail of looted armour on the base of Trajan's Column, early second century. Note that the helm at the bottom has a scale skirt.

8 A cavalryman from the *Stuttgart Psalter*, *c.* 830, showing a scale shirt to the knee with sleeves to the wrist. (Courtesy of the Würtemburg State Library)

9 Detail from the *Stuttgart Psalter*, *c.* 830. Note the clear demarkation between the corselet and skirt. (Courtesy of the Würtemburg State Library)

10 Steatite icon of Saints George and Theodore, Constantinople? Twelfth century. (State Historical Museum, Moscow. After Lazarev)

11 An example of Polish *karacena* parade armour. Second half of seventeenth century. (Polish Army Museum, Warsaw)

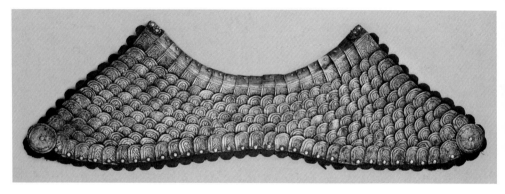

12 Scaled *culet* (rear skirt), Italy *c.* 1620. Wallace Collection. (By permission of the Trustees of the Wallace Collection)

13 Scaled buff-leather vambrace gauntlet, England, seventeenth century. (Royal Armouries Museum)

14 Full exterior view of the John Gregory Bourke armour, early to mid-nineteenth century (Collection of the Nebraska State Historical Society. Photograph courtesy of Peter Bleed)

15 Constructional detail of the John Gregory Bourke armour. (Photograph courtesy of Peter Bleed)

16 Cast members of a nineteenth-century production of the *Ring of the Niebelungen* wearing well made scale and mail armours.

17 Detail of a relief from Nimrud, Assyria, c.728 BCE. (British Museum)
18 Detail of a relief from Nimrud, Assyria, 865–60 BCE. (British Museum)

19 Detail of the reconstruction of the armour from Idalion, Cyprus, c. 500 BCE. (National Museum, Stockholm)

20 Rear view of Mars of Todi, fourth century BCE. (Vatican Etruscan Museum, Rome.)

21 Upper view of Mars of Todi, Etruscan, fourth century BCE. (Vatican Etruscan Museum, Rome)

22 Etruscan warriors, 400–350 BCE. (British Museum)

23 Three warrior gods, Palmyra, mid-first century CE. (Louvre)

24 Leather lamellar horse armour
panel from Dura Europos, mid-second
century CE. (Yale University Art Gallery,
Dura-Europos Collection)

25 Detail of a Chinese armour of the eighteenth century combining a Dura-Europos fabric body with later universal hanging form sleeves. (Royal Armouries Museum)

26 Detail of the horse armour on the relief of Khosroes II at Taq-i-Bustan, early-seventh century CE. (The Ernst Herzfeld papers, Freer Gallery of Art and Arthur M. Sackler Gallery Archives)

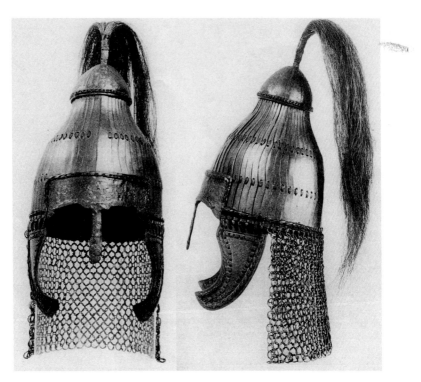

27 Reconstruction of the lamellar helm from Niederstotzingen, sixth century CE. (After Paulsen)

28 Christ before Pilate, from a Syriac manuscript, twelftth century. (© British Library Board, ms. Or 7170)

29 Detail of the Harbaville Triptych, Constantinople, tenth century. (Louvre)
30 Donor portrait of *Prôtospatharios* Iôannês from the *Adrianople Gospels*, 1007. (After Evan and Wixom)

31 Reconstruction of the parade outfit of *Prôtospatharios* Iôannês by the author.
32 Goliath, church of the Holy Cross, Aght'amar, Armenia, 915–19.

33 Detail from a manuscript of the *Shahnama* of Firdawsi, Tabriz, 1330–40. (Arthur M. Sackler Gallery, Smithsonian Institution, Washington, DC)

34 Detail from a manuscript of the *Shahnama* of Firdawsi, Shiraz. 1341. (Arthur M. Sackler Gallery, Smithsonian Institution, Washington, DC)

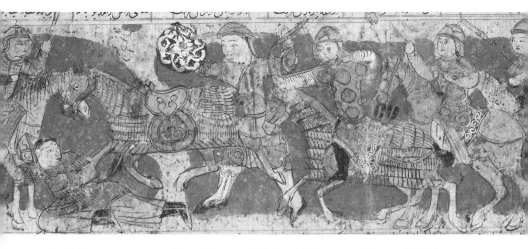

35 Detail from a manuscript of the *Shahnama* of Firdawsi, Shiraz, 1341. (Freer and Sackler Galleries Smithsonian Institution, Washington, DC)

36 Detail of a hypothetical strap and stud fastening on a reconstructed *klivanion* (*ill. 31*) by the author.

37 The author's
reconstruction of
a twelfth-century
elite infantry
harness.

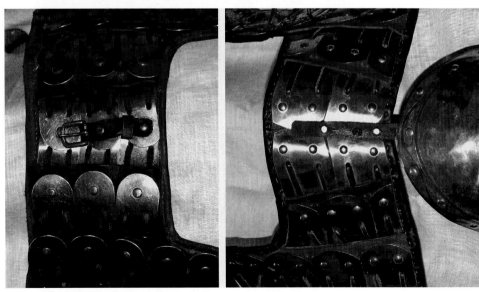

38 Details of hypothetical reconstructions of shoulder attachments for middle Byzantine
lamellar *klivania*. *Left*: strap and buckle. *Right*: strap and double stud with shoulder cop.

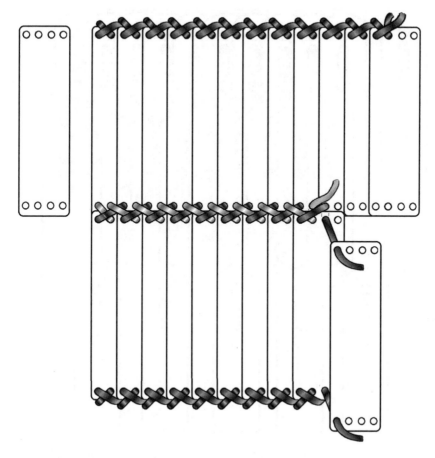

Fig. 15 Hypothetical lamellar reconstruction from Assyrian reliefs, seventh century BCE.

to precisely corroborate the construction. It is a form evidently related to some degree to the Hasanlu plate yet, in contrast to that, I have hypothesised four holes in my reconstruction because two holes alone would not allow a braided joint as the carvings show, while four close-set holes produces a denser binding that fully conceals the join in the manner shown in the figures. It is possible though that a braided construction similar to the one Thordeman hypothesised for the Amathus lamellar might have been used (*fig. 16*).

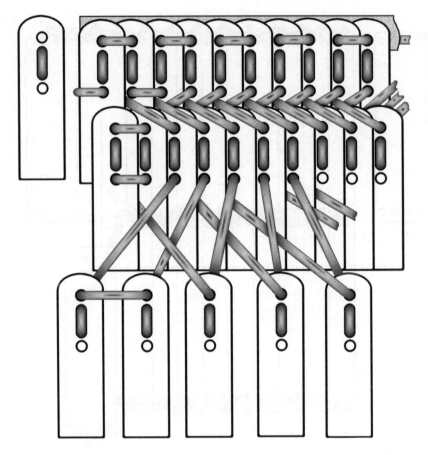

Fig. 16 Possible construction of the lamellar found at Amathus, Cyprus, fifth century BCE. Top edge and two succeeding rows.

The Swedish Cyprus Expedition recovered two deposits of bronze exterior small plate armour, one from Amathus, and the other at Idalion, both sites dated to the early fifth century BCE. Although they were completely disarticulated, without any traces of organic material, it seems most likely that they were both lamellar constructions. The Swedish Cyprus Expedition treats these finds in a somewhat contradictory manner. They suggest a braided assembly method for the Amathus material, which is possible (*figs 12.4, 16*),[III] yet which leaves a significant weakness in that having a lace pass between horizontally adjacent plates creates a step and

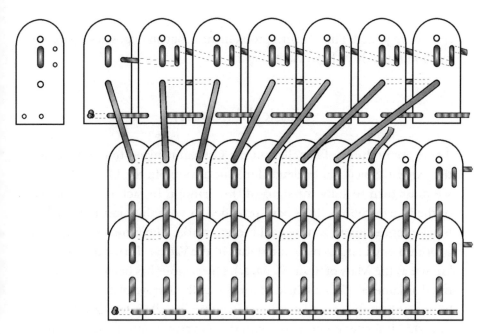

Fig. 17 A possible construction of the armour found at Idalion, Cyprus, fifth century BCE.

gap which might allow a point to lodge. That vulnerability may explain why almost half of every plate is hidden behind the row below, perhaps providing a second layer of defence in that case. The plates from Idalion are a remarkably diverse array of shapes and hole patterns, and without any traces of articulation it is virtually impossible to make a comprehensive hypothesis as to how it was assembled (*fig. 12.3a–h*). The Swedish Cyprus Expedition archaeologists proposed that the most common plates in the set (*fig. 12.3e–f*) could be assembled as a laced scale armour with no base garment.[112] A reconstruction was carried out shortly after its recovery, approximately embodying this notion, which remains on display in the National Museum, Stockholm (*ill. 19*).[113] While superficially attractive in that arrangement, the assembly would be improbably fragile. Nor is there any comparable evidence for purely laced scale construction in the West. More plausibly, Thordeman suggested that they were a lamellar.[114] What Thordeman's proposition lacked was a suggestion of how the rows were joined. This remains problematical, but an exposed suspension method might have been viable (*fig. 17*).

Classical Antiquity

There are no hints of lamellar on the Greek mainland to complement the extensive pictorial evidence for scale armour. In the Classical world we must turn to Italy for signs of this armour. In fact, the Etruscans of the fourth century BCE have provided us with the most remarkably precise representations in several bronze works. The most spectacular is a monumental larger-than-life statue in the Vatican Etruscan Museum known as the Mars of Todi (*ill. 20, 21*). The armour has been long recognised as lamellar.[115] The fabric of long, usually narrow, plates apparently bound only at the end is corroborated by similar, albeit less grand, works (*ill. 22*).[116] It invites comparison with the Assyrian group and the Hasanlu find, and doubtless came into use during the seventh century when Etruscan culture absorbed many Oriental influences. Closer inspection reveals that where they are not so degraded, the ridges between the rows on these armours are almost always marked with continuous diagonal striations, suggesting a wrapped binding like the proposed Hasanlu reconstruction (*fig. 14*).[117] An exception is found on both these examples, where the lowest binding only is in a herringbone pattern like the Assyrian reliefs. The fact that that binding secures plates which form a skirt free to move at the bottom is quite enough reason why the armourer would employ a more robust method of attachment than the spiral wrap used otherwise. These statues show the familiar form of the Classical cuirass, with the greater scale of Mars of Todi affording exceptional additional details. His corselet opens on the left side with three pairs of studs placed at the top under the armpit and then on the third rows to secure textile fastenings. Similar studs are paired on the ends of the shoulder straps and chest for further such fastenings (*ill. 20*). Unlike the other examples, Mars' shoulder straps are in a lamellar identical to the body at the front. The upper back panel to which the shoulder straps attach, in contrast, has lames of quite different proportions, with free-hanging projections to reinforce the ends of the junction between the body tube and the shoulder-piece (*ill. 21*). The standing panel protecting the back of the neck is a remarkable feature. What might these armours have been made of? These bronzes are themselves testament to the finely honed skills of Etruscan bronze-workers, as were the numerous solid bronze cuirasses of earlier times. By the fourth century BCE, however, iron had taken over for the manufacture of weapons. The larger the expanse of a sheet of metal, the relatively weaker it becomes, and the more vulnerable to being pierced. Hence, the unitary bronze cuirasses might have proven to be less effective than they had been. Furthermore, the flexibility of small plate armours means they yield to an attack, thereby reducing its effective power. Therefore, with improvements in weaponry it made defensive sense to go from solid breastplates to segmental armours, even when bronze remained the material. Yet, it is also possible that this change in armour construction might betoken a development towards iron being used for armour as well as weapons and tools. One thinks of the iron cuirass of Philip II of Macedon found at Vergina. That shows that smiths of the time could produce and manipulate relatively large masses of iron, but iron lamellar plates are a much more viable scale of work for non-royal armours.

The absorption of the Etruscan kingdoms into the Roman state resulted in the abandonment of many Etruscan cultural elements, evidently including the use of lamellar. It is not until the Age of Migrations brought about the fall of the western provinces of the Roman empire that we again see lamellar in use in Europe.

Late Antiquity

The Near East
There is, alas, little evidence for the Near East for many centuries following the latest of the Assyrian reliefs. From the second half of the third century BCE to the first half of the third century CE, the great power east of Rome was the Parthian empire under the Arsacid dynasty, which incorporated territory in modern-day Eastern Turkey, Iraq and Iran.

The region disputed between the Roman and Parthian empires provides a fine cluster of evidence for lamellar in the first and second centuries. A group of stone reliefs from Palmyra and its environs depict armoured figures, some with inscriptions indicating that they represent gods. They all wear corselets of narrow plates with substantial ridges between (*ill. 23*). The fabric is clearly of the same family as one of the Assyrian types and the Etruscan form, although the carvings are not detailed enough to indicate whether the binding is braided like the Assyrian or wrapped like the Etruscan. The structure of the corselets is very much in the Roman version of the Classical mode, with shoulder straps and tasseled *pteruges*. These reliefs range from the mid-first century into the second century.[118] Palmyra was incorporated into the Roman empire under Emperor Tiberius (14–37 CE), and over the following century became increasingly Romanised, leading, it seems clear, to this type of armour falling out of use.

The Parthian empire decayed in the late second century, and the power of the ruling dynasty was almost fatally compromised by severe defeats at Roman hands at the end of that century. Within the empire there were cultural differences between the Parthians in the west and the Persians in the east, which came to a head with the weakening of central power. In 224 the Persian vassal king Ardashir (I) rebelled; his defeat of the Parthian king Artabanus IV ushered in the Sassanian dynasty. The pictorial evidence for this period consists of large-scale stone reliefs depicting this conflict. These reliefs suggest that there were significant differences in military fashion between the two groups. Reliefs at Tang-i-Sarvak (probably from the second century) and Firuzabad show Persian warriors wearing mail, while Parthians wear long lamellar corselets. This is especially striking in the depiction of Ardashir defeating Artabanus at Firuzabad.[119] Unfortunately, these rock reliefs are not sufficiently detailed to allow us to guess what constructional fabric the Parthians used for their lamellar; however, the length of the corselets shown does preclude them being made of the narrow plate Assyrian form which we have seen from the surviving Palmyran sculptures from close to this period, because that construction is not sufficiently flexible to allow the manufacture of long garments.

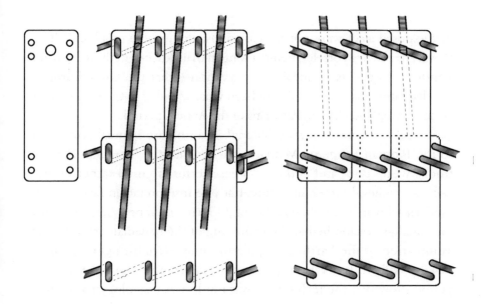

Fig. 18 Construction of the lamellar found at Dura-Europos, mid-third century. *Left,* outside.; *right,* inside.

Having consolidated their new state within existing boundaries, the Sassanian Persians soon went on the offensive outside them. The Roman city of Dura-Europos was an early victim, being besieged and destroyed in 256. That destruction created a treasure trove of archaeological material, much of it military. Among that were two triangular panels of leather lamellar (*ill. 24*). These have been conjectured to be thigh armour, but their size is much more consistent with them being horse armour. The construction of this lamellar is distinctive in that its suspension laces run entirely on the exterior of one side of the fabric (*fig. 18*). This arrangement has led some commentators to the conclusion that the armour was used with the suspension laces on the inside.[120] That is possible, but comparable examples suggest not. Both the Royal Armouries Museum and the Metropolitan Museum both hold full harnesses of this form of lamellar, also in leather, with all the suspension laces on the outside (*ill. 25*). Admittedly, both suits originate from the Far East, and are very much later than the Dura-Europos siege, but provide ample evidence that exposed laces were not seen as an insurmountable problem.[121] The Royal Armouries corselet, being a longer-than-knee-length horseman's armour, also points to another observation – that the Dura-Europos lamellar fabric may very well have been what was used in the long cavalry armours employed by the Parthians of the Arsacid period.

Several centuries later, the *Stratêgikon*, a military manual attributed to the Roman Emperor Maurice, tells us that the Sassanian Persian troops wore '*zavai* and *lôrikia*'.[122] These terms are used rather erratically in medieval Greek literature, but one interpretation favoured by modern scholars is 'padding and mail'.[123] That would be in keeping with the paradigm established at the beginning of the Sassanian era. Yet their assimilation of the Parthian population must have brought lamellar-making skills with it. Various pieces of evidence from the late Sassanian period show that the technology was not lost. Archaeology has turned up several collections of lames. Qasr-i-abu Nasr yielded a deposit of iron and bronze lames in the proportions of thirteen iron plates to one bronze (*fig. 12.7*). The group is regarded as being Late Antique, although it has not been precisely dated.[124] The lames are quite small, about 65mm by 15mm, and, as far as could be established, are variable in shape, but all are punched with the simplest solid lacing pattern that is seen elsewhere in the sixth century (*fig. 19*). This group is not large. With its small size of plates, it might have made a helmet skirt, but with such an inflexible lacing it would not serve that purpose well, so its original use remains uncertain. Another very small cluster of lames was found at Togolok Tepe by Russian excavators dated by stratigraphy to the early seventh century.[125] These plates might not have been recognised as lamellar at all but for retaining some binding. They are narrow, with just one hole near each end through which a cord wrapped them together in rows. While they bear some resemblance to the Etruscan/Hasanlu group, with so few holes, the construction is very much cruder and less functional than these and other types of lamellar existing in the same period and region. The likelihood is that this piece was a hasty improvisation which reinvented the wheel at a very clumsy level, rather than anything which grew out of an established suite of knowledge and skill. Manifestly, the Persians of that era did have an established suite of knowledge and skill as makers of

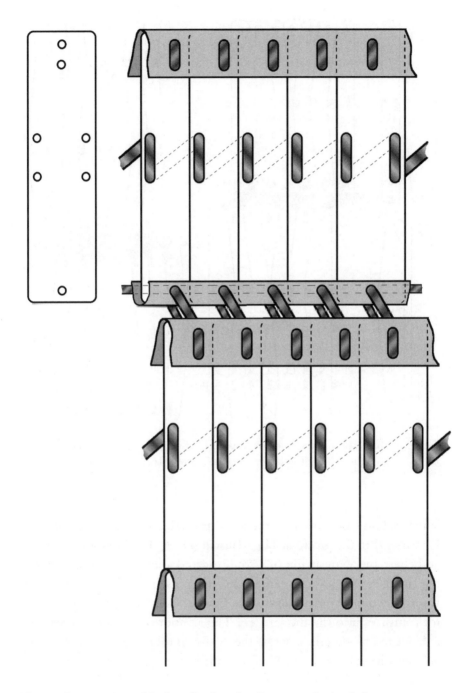

Fig. 19 Construction of the lamellar found at Cartagena, Spain, sixth century.

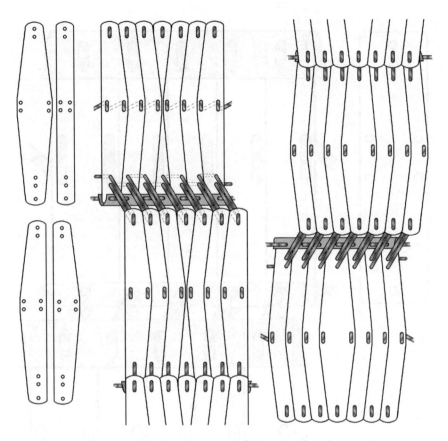

Fig. 20 Construction of the horse armour of Khosroes II, early seventh century. Left: chest. Right: crinet. Top lames – centres. Lower lames – main fabric.

lamellar. This can be seen in the armour carried by the mount of Shah Khosroes II in the grotto at Taq-i-Bustan (*ill. 26*). The horse's neck-piece and chest-piece are made of a sophisticated and finely finished hanging lamellar, which is the earliest surviving instance of the form which was to become standard across the Levant, Caucasus and Central Asia for centuries into the modern era. The armour of Khosroes' horse has a dedicated binding lace across the centre of each row (and very probably another along the hidden bottom edge of the row, for stability), and a single dedicated suspension lace for each plate. Both sets of laces have very little exposure to attack, thereby making this form very robust.

The complex and consistent three-dimensional shaping shown on the lames of this harness further make it clear that it is made of metal. The lames of the chest-piece overlap forward to the centre front, and upward, as expected (*fig. 20, left*). The lames of the neck-piece, however, overlap rearward from the centre, and are suspended inverted to facilitate the necessary expansion down to the shoulders, just as can be seen on late medieval Western horse armours of plate. Given the quality and sophistication of this construction, it is remarkable that the Sassanians had not applied the technique to arming their men, but perhaps the explanation is that it was a new form at this time and unproven. Archaeology has, as yet, offered us no corroboration of this development.

South-eastern Europe and Crimea

Historical literary sources give a wide array of names for the groups of people who surged into Europe in the Age of Migrations – Avars, Huns, Goths, Lombards. The literature is written in Latin and Greek from the perspective of the settled society, not the migratory peoples. It is never clear, therefore, just how the literary classifications resembled actual ethnic divisions that those various peoples would have recognised. Archaeology has yielded a great deal of material from the migratory people but, of course, that does not come with explicit ethnic labels, although archaeologists and art historians will often claim that art styles they feel they can define virtually function as such. In terms of exterior small plate armour, however, archaeological finds from the Crimea to southern Germany have returned plates with such similar characteristics that they can reasonably be attributed to a common cultural milieu which is conventionally called 'Avar'. The scale armours from this source were discussed in the previous section (see pages 38–9), but the lamellar is very much more copious and significant.

The two largest finds were from grave 12a at Niederstotzingen and at Krefeld-Gellep in southern Germany where in both cases a warrior was buried with a complete harness. The Niederstotzingen corselet was very successfully recovered and published by Paulsen, who was

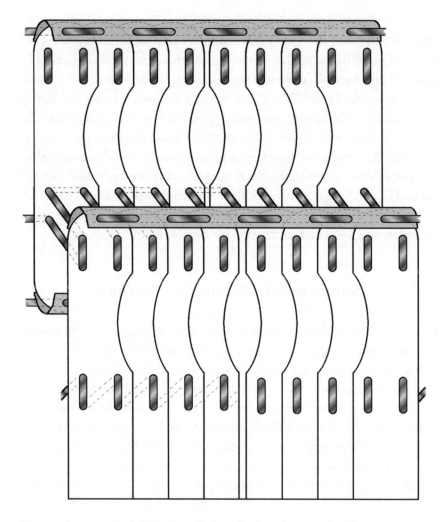

Fig. 21 Construction of Avar lamellar based primarily upon that from Krefeld-Gellep showing primary and lower edge rows, *c.* 540.

sufficiently confident of his conclusions as to construct a replica.[126] The Krefeld-Gellep situation was not so successful, with a serious transportation accident between the site and the laboratory causing irrecoverable damage before it could be fully studied.[127]

The common characteristics of lames from these sites is that they are approximately rectangular with rounded corners, between four and six times as long as they are wide, and with one edge indented. Scattered lames with such characteristics, and sometimes identical forms, have been found across south-eastern Europe[128] and in the Crimea.[129] The Niederstotzingen harness was made up of five different lames tailored to particular functions in the armour, with three occurring in mirrored form. Seven different plates were identified in the Krefeld-Gellep corselet, with four being mirrored and the remaining three being straight plates intended to bridge the change in direction of the lateral overlap (*figs 12, 8a–e and 21*).

A careful examination had been made of the Krefeld-Gellep armour before it was lifted, and that is enough to indicate that it had much the same overall form as the Niederstotzingen corselet. This construction consisted of a torso-piece made up of six or seven horizontal rows with a row approximately at right angles passing over each shoulder, and a skirt of four or five horizontal rows. In both armours the rows that enclosed the chest were in one piece, with an opening on the right side secured with straps and buckles, while the skirt had a one-piece waistband fastened with a buckle supporting two skirt panels separated front and back. Paulsen indicates that the chest-piece of the Niederstotzingen armour was solid-laced, while the skirts were hanging.[130] Paulsen's reconstruction has the shoulder bands set precisely at right angles to the body rows, running from armpit level front to back, with two short rows between them to cover the upper chest and back. On a purely practical level, such a construction is not entirely plausible, for the entire weight of the harness would then rest on the inner edges of the shoulder bands, pressing them painfully into the muscles. The pieces I believe to be the shoulder bands of the Krefeld-Gellep armour (which were less damaged in the accident) are very much shorter – of a suitable length to run between the top of the chest and back. They are also stepped in a way that adds a little freedom of movement at the front while providing more protection at the back (*fig. 22*). My reconstruction also sets them at a suitable angle to distribute the weight across the width of the bands. In addition to the practical consideration, there are detached plates of Avar form which have holes that are supernumerary to the required standard bindings and which might have been used to make such tailored

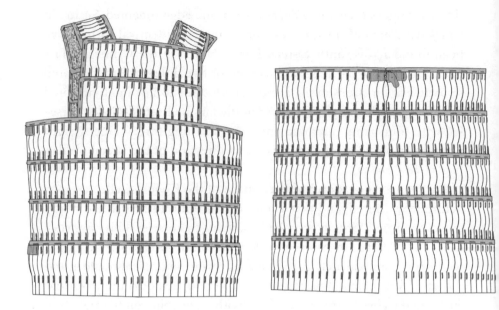

Fig. 22 Reconstruction of an Avar lamellar corselet, based upon the Krefeld–Gellep find.

attachments. With so much information lost due to the accident, any reconstruction of the Krefeld–Gellep harness must be largely speculative. It seemed reasonable to infer that the plates with no hole at one end (*fig. 12.8c*) would form a lower edge as the lower set of holes would in that situation serve purely as a secure binding, rendering a further edge binding superfluous.[131] Yet there was a group of that form which were curiously curved and presented a particular conundrum (*fig. 12.8d*). Continuing the previous inference, I have conjectured that if the curved lames formed the bottom of the chest-piece, the skirt might be buckled on over it, preserving the lamellar paradigm of rows overlapping upward, with the bulge created by the curvature of the plates preventing the skirt from riding up too far. Whereas I was able to test the shoulder arrangement with a mock-up, testing this theory could only be done by building a full set in metal, a project for there was no time during the preparation of this volume. So, if any reader takes on that project, I would be pleased to hear of the result.

A remarkable accompaniment to the Niederstotzingen corselet was a lamellar helmet. Long, narrow, tapering strips ran from a brow-plate with nasal at the front and a narrow edging band around the remaining circumference to a prominent dome cap with a plume holder. The lames were bound together at one point above the brow-plate and two points elsewhere in addition to the ends. Below the skull, protection was provided by cheek-pieces and a mail skirt (*ill. 27*). Fragments of comparable lamellar helmets were found at Kertch, dated to the sixth century, and Nocera Umbra and Castel Trosino in Italy, both Lombardic sites, dated to the seventh century.[132] In fact, it has been noted that lamellar helmet construction is a very widespread technique which is, perhaps not surprisingly, as old as lamellar body armour.[133] Nevertheless, it may seem curious that lamellar helmet construction was employed in this period and locality. These people certainly knew of more solid methods of helmet construction. The cemetery at Krefeld-Gellep contained a fully riveted spangenhelm of a similar period to the lamellar corselet found there. It is also notable that further lamellar helmet construction continued into relatively modern times.[134] The explanation may lie in the way the production can be diffused and carried out using fewer tools. A riveted helmet must be made from start to finish by a skilled metal-worker, who has not only the techniques, but also specialised tools such as the anvil stake needed to set the rivets, especially near the apex. In contrast, once a smith has forged the pieces, a lamellar helmet can be assembled by another labourer with few tools. The smaller quantity of iron tooling needed must be a distinct advantage for any nomadic or semi-nomadic lifestyle, and even in a sedentary society the division of labour could significantly speed up production.

The Middle Ages

The Roman Empire after the fall of the western provinces (Byzantion)
The precise chronology of the assimilation of lamellar into mainstream

Roman use and the technological developments that flow from that remains obscure. The *Stratêgikon*, a military manual from around 602, does not contain any certain reference to lamellar being used for the soldiers. It says that the armour for the troops is to be *zavai*. As noted in Part 1 (pages 37–8), the term seems predominantly to mean mail, but exterior small plate armour of one sort or another is possible. More clearly, the cavalry horses are to have 'breast-pieces of iron or quilting'. The 'breast-pieces of iron' may refer to scale, as seen in earlier use like at Dura-Europos, but are probably more likely to allude to lamellar, as in both Dura-Europos and the contemporary relief of Khosroes II (*ill. 26*).

The next cluster of military literature is several centuries later, in the tenth century. Lamellar features prominently in the explosion of Byzantine military literature of that century. The *Taktika* of Emperor Leo, and the closely related *Syllogê Taktikôn*, both from the very beginning of the century, recommend *klivania* (lamellar corselets) of iron or horn.[135] In one place, Leo states that the *klivania* should be 'polished and bright', confirming the preference for iron.[136] These stipulations are applied to horses as much as to the troops. One reference in the *Taktika* allows the possibility of *klivania* covering only the front of the body, a very understandable expedient in the given context of naval warfare, for not only are the hand-to-hand engagements much more limited, but a chest-only armour would be much easier to discard in the event of a man going overboard.[137] The *Composition on Warfare* of Nikêforos Fôkas from the third quarter of the tenth century (and the *Taktika* of Nikêforos Ouranos, which was based upon it) give some more information on the soldier's *klivanion*, indicating that it is just a breast and back, with the sleeves and skirts as separate units, just as shown in the art of the time (*ills 28–30*).[138] Later, Fôkas says the equestrian *klivanion* should be made of ox hide and extend to the animal's knees. The difference in materials for the horse lamellar may also imply a difference in construction, as discussed below. It is primarily pictorial material that elucidates the types of lamellar being used in and around Constantinople prior to 1204. The period from the mid-seventh century to the late ninth century is sometimes called the 'Dark Age of Byzantion', as a combination of external attacks and internal divisions radically curtailed all forms of cultural production, especially in the visual arts. Thereafter, pictorial material does not become plentiful again until the eleventh century. Several very similar artworks of the tenth century, the Borradile Triptych in the British Museum, the Harbaville Triptych in the Louvre Museum and an ivory panel in the Metropolitan Museum, present the earliest indication within this period.[139] The armour on these various warrior saints resembles inverted large scales more than familiar forms of lamellar (*ill. 29*). The resolution to that improbable scenario may be found in the example of the armour found at Turfan in Turkestan, whose lame shape more resembles scale more than other types of lamellar (*fig. 23*). With the only comparable material coming from so far beyond the eastern and northern borders of the empire, it is not clear how this form was brought to the city. Eleventh- and twelfth-century artworks offer clearer answers, especially when corroborated against the sole piece of metropolitan archaeological evidence. The better-executed pictures show lames with parallel edges which have a clear top curvature, proving that they do not overlap laterally. The lames

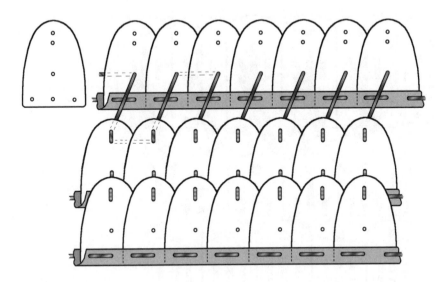

Fig. 23 Construction of the lamellar found at Turfan, Turkestan, tenth to fourteenth centuries.

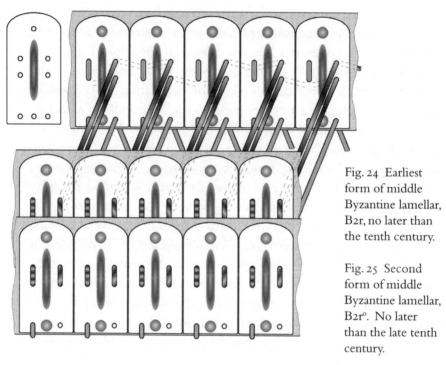

Fig. 24 Earliest
form of middle
Byzantine lamellar,
B2r, no later than
the tenth century.

Fig. 25 Second
form of middle
Byzantine lamellar,
B2r°. No later
than the late tenth
century.

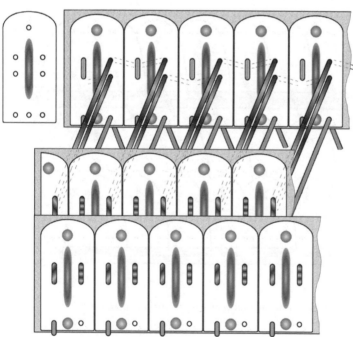

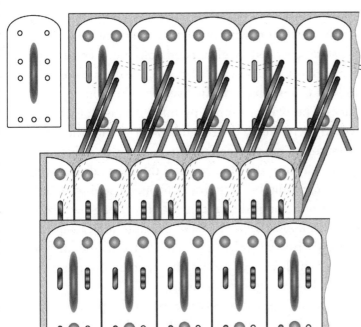

Fig. 26 Third
form of middle
Byzantine lamellar,
B2r2°. By 1007.

Fig. 27 Fourth
form of middle
Byzantine lamellar,
B4r°. Later
eleventh and
twelfth centuries.

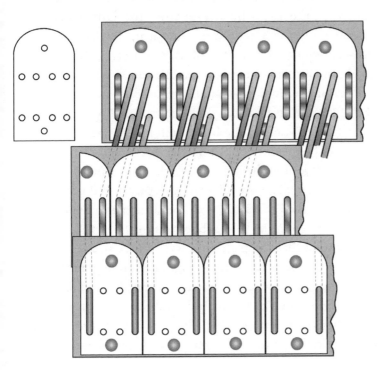

have one or two dots at the top, with two or four vertical lines lower down, and the rows are separated by plain bands, often in a contrasting colour. The dots are rivets securing the plates to a leather band, as is confirmed by finds of plates which retain rivets,[140] while the lines are the suspension laces. The primary form, by inference, is B2r (*fig. 24*). B2r^{offset} (*fig. 25*) would therefore be the secondary form with the lames offset from one row to the next by half a plate in order to reduce any danger that might result from the alignment of the intervals between the lames. B2r2 (*fig. 26*) would be the tertiary form, created to reduce the possibility that an acute-angled thrust might lift the edge of a lame and penetrate. This is the most securely dated example, appearing in a donor portrait explicitly labelled as having been painted in 1007 (*ills 30, 31*). B4r° (*fig. 27*) is the final form of the twelfth century, doubling the number of suspension laces for greater durability.

Obviously in the pictorial sources only the external, upper portion of each row is visible. The B2r form is corroborated by an archaeological find in Constantinople. The excavations in the Great Palace precinct conducted in the 1930s by a team from the University of St Andrews in Scotland found a deposit of armour in the destruction layer, which was securely dated by a coin of Manuel I (1143–80) fused to it. Unfortunately, the primary records of the excavation were mislaid, and the Archaeological Museum in Istanbul similarly has no record of the location of the armour itself at the time of writing.[141] We are left, therefore, to make a guess based on the brief published description and grainy photograph.[142] The quantity of plates (over 200) is sufficient for a complete corselet. The layout of the holes as described is identical to the visible part of B2r (*fig. 12.12*). The overall form is reconstructed from the description published by the excavators, with the shaded area being the distinct fragment illustrated in the sole publication for hole placement. The excavators recorded that the plates occurred in six sizes ranging from 30–60mm wide by about twice that long. The subtle graduation of plate sizes would suggest some sophisticated tailoring. Lack of further data due to the disappearance of the records and the armour unfortunately makes further analysis impossible. The presence of three holes along the lower edge referred to by the report leads to the inference that these lamellars had an interior supplementary suspension lace. This practice may have persisted with B4r°.

This Byzantine construction with lames affixed side by side to leather backing confers a significant saving in plate materials, and in weight when iron is used. When hide is used for the lames, as mentioned for horse armour, those savings would not be enough as to justify the additional work, and leather for the backing. Hence, it is probable that hide lamellar horse armour was made using one of the simpler and more widespread methods of construction, such as the universal hanging form (*fig. 28; ill. 25 sleeves*) or Turfan (*fig. 23*).

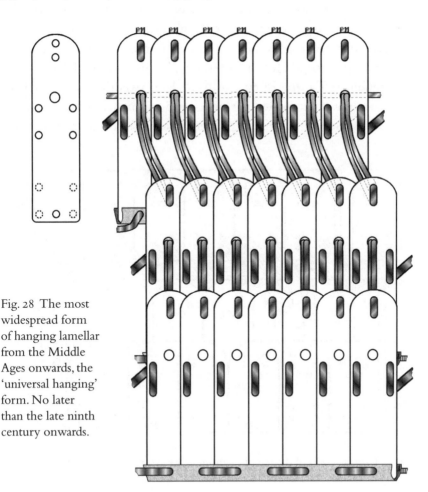

Fig. 28 The most widespread form of hanging lamellar from the Middle Ages onwards, the 'universal hanging' form. No later than the late ninth century onwards.

One picture from the first decade of the eleventh century presents a singular construction not attested in any other source. It is the parade *klivanion* worn by Emperor Basil II in the triumphal portrait that forms the frontispiece of his psalter. It seems to be a banded form, but apparently laced solid *(fig. 29)*. Without anything to compare it to, it cannot be definitively said that this was a unique, and perhaps experimental, creation for the emperor, but the fact that there is nothing like it among the quite common depictions of middle Byzantine warriors suggests that it cannot have had much wider use.

In the later eleventh and twelfth centuries there are no equivalent technical documents to the military manuals of the tenth century. The references to military equipment in the historical literature of the period are necessarily less precise, and the convention of 'Atticism' applied by the more pretentious authors often entailed deliberate obfuscation of such details.[143] Writing of events in the later twelfth century, Nikêtas Khoniatês mentions 'scaled garments' and 'garments of iron plates'.[144] The words used in Khoniatês' impeccable Classicising style (*folis* and

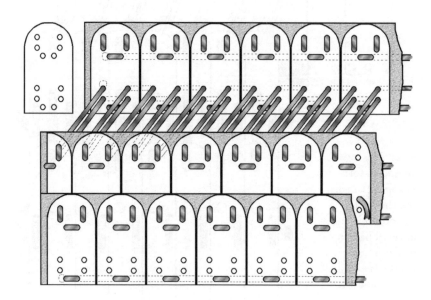

Fig. 29 Construction of the parade armour of Emperor Basil II, *c.* 1010.

folidôtos) meant scale armour in antiquity, but in the twelfth century would have covered lamellar as well.

When first formulating theories about the technological developments in middle Byzantine lamellar as represented in the art of the period, I hypothesised a transition from the universal form of hanging lamellar (*fig. 28; fig. 12.10*) to the banded, riveted two-lace form (B2r) via one hypothetical intermediate step.[145] While the hole pattern was similar, that transition would have required a total reallocation of hole usage. Those holes that had been binding would become suspension, and those which had been suspension would become attachment. The scale of that change was always questionable. Another complication in that theory was that the only evidence for the universal form of hanging lamellar in the West was from Birka, at a later date than the evidence suggests for the commencement of the Byzantine evolution, and was of a style indicating a more eastern influence, rather than pointing to a source which could have influenced the Romans. The form of the copious and consistent Avar lamellar discussed previously now shows that that theory was incorrect. The Avar pattern converts into B2r much more directly, with a small reduction in the number of holes, but with no variation in hole distribution, nor in hole use (*fig. 31*). Furthermore, Byzantion had direct contact with the Avars in the sixth and seventh centuries, and the Byzantines are recorded in their own words as copying a great many Avar practices among their soldiery, and especially the cavalry.[146] Clearly, the Avar connection is a much more plausible starting point for the introduction of lamellar into the Roman army.

In developing the Avar lamellar pattern, Constantinopolitan practice is almost certain to have passed through the phase shown on the Church of the Holy Cross at Aght'amar in Armenia. There, there is a standing full-length picture of Goliath, wearing a lamellar corselet which has lames punched in the Avar pattern, although straight-edged, and ranged side by side with no lateral overlap (*ill. 32*). This indicates that it must be fully backed, like the later Byzantine banded forms, but it is shown as having a strip wrapped over the edge, just as the Avar pieces had, yet with that wrapping riveted through at the centre top (and probably bottom) of each lame through the same hole as had been used for lacing the edging

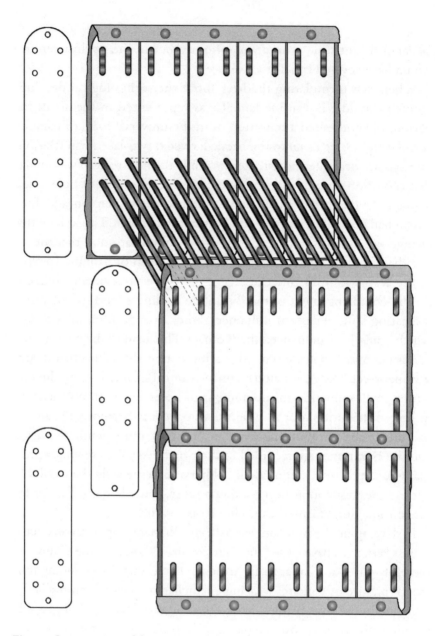

Fig. 30 Construction of the armour of the Goliath of Aght'amar, Armenia, 911–13. Showing primary and bottom rows.

on in the earlier form (*fig. 30; compare fig. 21*). There was probably a lost intermediate form, perhaps in the eighth century, which had the lames fully backed and edged, but with the backing/edging still laced on and not yet riveted. Armenia's long relationship with Constantinople had been fraught for many centuries.[147] The Church of the Holy Cross had been built during one of the periods when it had attained its independence. It would be a very plausible symbolic reference in that context for Goliath to be depicted as a Byzantine soldier confronted and cast down by Armenia in the guise of David.[148] In view of the rate of change implied by the eleventh- and twelfth-century Byzantine pictures, the date of the construction of the Church of the Holy Cross, 915–19, could well be accurate for this phase of lamellar development; albeit, perhaps, late in the phase.

The atrocities of the Fourth Crusade had a devastating effect upon Byzantine society. That the Rômiosi were able to regroup and claw their way back to recover Constantinople in 1261 is a feat of cultural resilience surpassing any other in recorded history. Yet a great deal was irrevocably lost, and it is evident that the production of lamellar was one of those losses. Palaiologian religious art, virtually the only source material there is from the period, features many warrior saints. They are all clad in more or less fanciful versions of armour, among which some people have sought to find lamellar. Certainly some of the patterning on those armours is clearly derived from earlier depictions of lamellar, yet what makes it plain that the artists did not comprehend what they were depicting is the facts that the patterns are themselves distorted, and are applied in peculiar orientations such as diagonal or radial. It is possible to conjecture that the radial arrangement was influenced by the so-called 'mirror armours' that were becoming established across the region. As discussed in the Introduction, it is possible to build something resembling such an armour, but doing so is the best verification of its falsehood. Not only does it require much more labour than a mirror armour, for example, but the radial segmental structure has great vulnerability to thrusts from the side sliding between the layers.

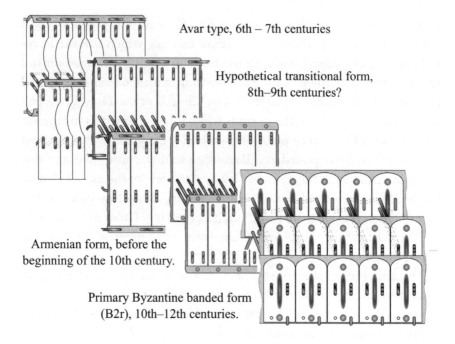

Avar type, 6th – 7th centuries

Hypothetical transitional form,
8th–9th centuries?

Armenian form, before the
beginning of the 10th century.

Primary Byzantine banded form
(B2r), 10th–12th centuries.

Fig. 31 Evolutionary sequence from Avar to the first form of middle Byzantine lamellar, B2r.

The Caucasus

Georgia is the other nation in the Byzantine Commonwealth which presents us with a great wealth of pictures of warrior saints conventionally dated in the tenth to twelfth centuries. It should be noted once again, however, that these are religious pictures somewhat derivative of Constantinople and to some degree constrained by iconographic conventions. In contrast to the Metropolis, very, very few of the surviving Georgian representations of the warrior saints are executed as manuscript illuminations or other finely detailed polychrome media. The greatest number occur in embossed metal, with some frescos. These art forms were the province of lay craftsmen, rather than the monastic milieu of manuscript art, which might sometimes have been detached

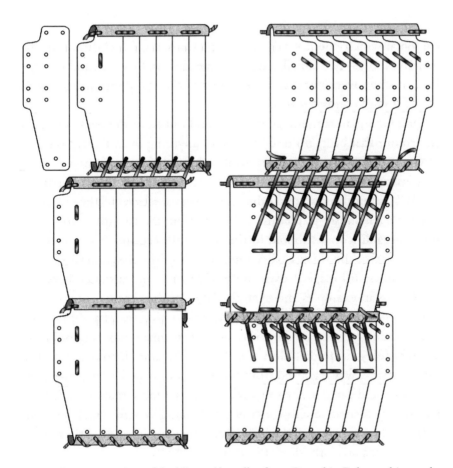

Fig. 32 Reconstruction of the 'C type' lamellar from Gomel in Belarus, thirteenth century. *Left*, outside; *right*, inside.

from contact with secular life, yet this hypothetically more socially engaged production context does not manifest in greater realism. On the contrary, Georgian pictures of exterior small plate armours are often very garbled. Frequently what one sees is a plate style and orientation derived from scale construction, but with the surface patterning copied from lamellar as shown in Byzantine pictures, or based upon them. The surface patterning of a whole corselet is sometimes faithful to the Constantinopolitan precedents for lamellar, albeit upside-down, but it, too, is more often garbled, even when the plate orientation and overlap are in the standard manner for lamellar. Without archaeological evidence which could verify such depictions, the conclusion must be that Byzantine-style lamellar was not prevalent in Georgia, and that the lay craftsmen were not directly exposed to the real item sufficiently to depict it with consistent accuracy.[149]

One Georgian warrior saint does stand out from the pack, showing an armour that bears no resemblance to anything from Byzantion. The St George of Jakhunderi, dated to the eleventh century, shows rows of very narrow plates with no surface detail, separated by narrow, textured bands. Tsurtsumia notes two other Georgian sources which he says show this type, a manuscript picture said to be from the twelfth century and the Labsqaldi icon attributed to the thirteenth century.[150] The external appearance of the form is very reminiscent of the Assyrian/Etruscan/ Palmyran traditions, but over the gulf of time and distance between the Georgian examples and even the latest of those earlier pictures, no continuity may be credibly proposed. These pictures may represent a reinvention of a very similar form, but Tsurtsumia reasonably points to an archaeological find at Gomel in Belarus. A large deposit of plates in three variants was retrieved from what was construed as an armourer's workshop and dated to the thirteenth century. One variant has a distinctive shape, created to allow a concealed lacing system which presents entirely blank faces on all the lames between edging bands, as those various Georgian artworks show (*fig. 12.15; fig. 32*).[151]

Europe

As discussed in Part 1, the most plausible evidence for the survival of exterior small plate armour in medieval Europe is for the use of scale armour among the Carolingian Franks. The *Stuttgart Psalter* of around 830 (which provides such copious and accurate depictions of scale armour) contains a single picture of a short corselet patterned with squares, some containing dots, which has been interpreted as lamellar, accompanied by a scale skirt.[152] The patterning does not resemble any coherent depiction of lamellar; in fact, it is closer to Byzantine quilting patterns.[153] As the man is fleeing an avenging spirit, it is more plausible to think that his arming, which had progressed as far as the scaled skirt, had been interrupted. (Scaled skirts alone are visible elsewhere in the manuscript. See the longer discussion in Part 1, on pages 39–43.) The fact that the harness which supports the skirt is visible, extending up almost to the man's chest, is further reason to think that the patterning on the man's chest is not meant to be armour.

Excavations of an early eleventh-century site at Lake Paladru in south-eastern France recovered a scattering of small arms fragments (arrow and javelin heads) and a sword pommel. Having extrapolated extravagantly from those few implements to the idea that this was a community of 'warrior-farmers',[154] the archaeologists decided that a few curious paired iron plates about 50mm square joined by a single bifurcated rivet in the centre must be remnants of armour. Their reconstruction to that end was of a '*broigne* of plates', a leather jerkin with the metal fixed to the outside. As discussed in the Introduction, the *broigne* of plates is a thoroughly unconvincing theory in any circumstances, and especially in the case of plates with a single rivet. No better is the proposition that the plates were from a Byzantine-style riveted lamellar.[155] The plates are of an entirely unsuitable shape for that application, and lack any hint of lacing holes.

It must be concluded that there is no persuasive evidence to suggest that in north-western Europe the use of lamellar survived the dissipation of the Avar culture, nor was it reintroduced by contact with the East as the period progressed.

Scandinavia

A certain coterie of re-enactors is very keenly committed to the notion that there was such a thing as 'Viking lamellar'; that is to say, lamellar made by, and used widely by, the Norse.[156] The evidence by no means supports this idea. It is true that a small quantity of lamellar was found on the island of Birka in modern-day Sweden, which had been a major town prior to its destruction around 970. This find was, however, very scanty and fragmentary, and has been misrepresented. Insofar as more or less complete plates could be identified from Birka, there are five types of significantly differing sizes, shapes and hole patterns. Only three are actually lames (*fig. 12.10*). The other two types are clearly scales rather than lames, contrary to Thordeman's classification (*fig. 11, type 3.5 and type 4.12*). While substantially differing plate forms can very occasionally be found in a single corselet, it is more likely that the three types of lamellar plates were from disparate armours. Furthermore, the total quantity, even if one makes the rash assumption that every fragment represents a entire plate, irrespective of plate type, is not sufficient to make even half a basic chest-plate. The pieces were found in the remains of a burned building which the archaeologists dubbed 'the armoury', for no reason other than the presence of this armour. It cannot be assumed that such a portion would be left behind in the final cataclysm if it had been in anything like a functional state. It is far more likely that this was a collection of scrap metal for recycling. No other Scandinavian archaeology of the Viking era (793–1066) has yielded anything to corroborate this find.

The Norse sagas do very occasionally include the term *spangabrynja*, a word which can be translated as 'splint armour' or 'plates armour', with all the attendant imprecision of such expressions. It is undoubtedly the term that Vikings who travelled eastwards would have coined to refer to both the lamellar and scale armours they encountered in Russia and beyond, yet its appearance in the sagas cannot necessarily be taken as indicating either one of those armours specifically. Those tales were an oral tradition which did not even begin to be recorded until the last decades of the twelfth century, long after the Viking age had ended, and the process of conversion to text took somewhat more than a century. It is a known feature of oral transmission that material details may be sporadically updated in order to make the narrative more familiar to an audience, and that that process continued as the sagas were committed to parchment. Armour is one area in which the updating process is most readily discerned, and *spangabrynja* features in that explicitly. For example, in the *Laexdaela Saga*, which covered events from the ninth to eleventh centuries but was written down in the thirteenth century, one warrior wears a panoply in which a *spangabrynja* accompanies a helmet with a brim the width of the breadth of a hand.[157] That helmet can immediately be recognised as a typical thirteenth-century kettle hat. In that context, this *spangabrynja* must be taken to be one of the coats of plates which had come into use in that century. The other few occurrences of *spanga-brynja* are less clear, but can no more be taken to date from the Viking era, or to mean either form of exterior small plate armour, rather than a later coat of plates.

The 'Viking lamellar' partisans will also invoke the find at Wisby in support of their theory. Three factors negate that expedient. The simplest is the date of the battle. 1361 is well beyond the bounds of the Viking age. The nature of the armour as buried is still more significant. There were several deposits scattered across the three mass graves. Most were so damaged and decayed that little can be said of them. One, however, designated 'Armour 25', was sufficiently well preserved to tell us a lot. Significantly, it was not deposited as lamellar – it had been reconstructed as a coat of plates, with leather on the outside and coarse cloth on the inside. This covering had been riveted into place with a complete disregard for its remaining characteristics as lamellar, and with a degree of crudity Thordeman considered noteworthy.[158] The armour had already been significantly damaged before the renovation, but had not been fully dismantled. Within, the covering rows were still fastened together with lacing here and there, and retaining leather edgings *(fig. 33)*. The mounting onto leather served to replace the lacing between the rows, with some rows being inserted reversed from their original position. Hence, the armour must have had a significant prehistory prior to the battle. Proponents of the 'Viking lamellar' thesis may seize upon that observation to claim it as being handed down from the Viking era, but, once again, its original construction resists this interpretation. The plate form and assembly are entirely different to the most prevalent form of medieval lamellar, which is the type found at Birka – the universal form of hanging lamellar *(fig. 28)*. Rather, Wisby Armour 25 is most consistent, both in its fabric and form of harness, with the type which was already in the process of being superseded in Late Antiquity. In both respects it is less sophisticated than the Krefeld-Gellep/Niederstotzingen group, while in plate form and assembly it is virtually identical to that found at Cartagena *(fig. 19)*. In that context, one possible explanation for all these observations is that in their desperate quest to make up the extreme

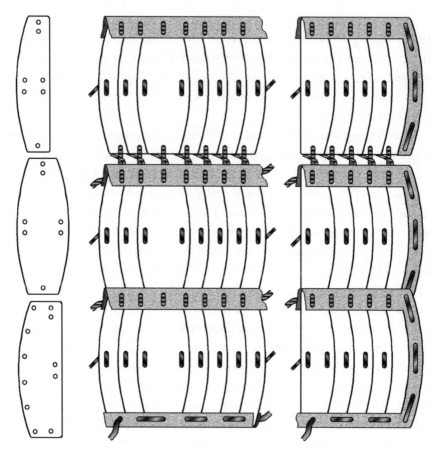

Fig. 33 Construction of Armour 25 from Wisby.

deficiency of armour, the fourteenth-century 'Home Guard' of Wisby raided well-preserved early Migration Era tombs, hastily remedying the deterioration by conversion into brigandine form. The basic solid-laced lamellar construction does recur in archaeology in a closer temporal context, but rather further away, in a Mesopotamian find of around the start of the thirteenth century (see pages 99–101). That is a period in which Scandinavians are known to have been active in the Crusading movement, so another possible hypothesis is that Swedish Crusaders brought lamellar shirts back with them. Those lamellar shirts might then have spent the next 150 years or so mouldering in Wisby churches as quasi-religious relics, before being pressed into service. That scenario could probably better explain the state of preservation evident in Wisby Armour 25; yet, even if true, the facts would still remain that the origins of the armour were not in Scandinavia, nor within the Viking period.

In summary, while a few individual Norsemen collected pieces of both types of exterior small plate armour as souvenirs on their travels and brought them back to Scandinavia, there was no such thing that could be properly be called 'Viking lamellar' or, indeed, 'Viking scale armour'.

Russia

Russian archaeological evidence for exterior small plate armour is dominated by scale. The notable exception to this rule is the discovery at Gomel in Belarus of what has been taken to be an armourer's workshop of the thirteenth century.[159] A large deposit of lames were found in five variants. Three variants (designated 'type A' by the archaeologists) were of the universal hanging form (*fig. 28*) virtually identical to those found at Birka (*fig. 12.10a–c*). The other two variants are quite distinctive. Both have concealed suspension lacing systems.[160] In addition to that, 'type B' has a fully concealed row lacing system which would result in there being nothing but metal visible on the surface. The scalloped edges of the lames are curved downward in order to cover the gap created by the laces lying between the plates (*fig. 12.14; fig. 34*). Gomel 'type C' presents an external appearance very much like the ancient forms from Assyria and Etruria, with closely spaced, straight-edged plates with no visible lacing running between bound edges (*fig. 32*). The construction of Gomel type C begins with the assembly of rows with leather edge bindings in the manner of the Late Antique forms.[161] The second stage, installing the suspension lace and the internal row binding, is then done simultaneously a lame at a time, with the suspension lace preceding the binding lace. As both internal laces pass through two plates, installing either one continuously would prevent the implementation of the other. These Gomel types are clearly related to forms illustrated from sources

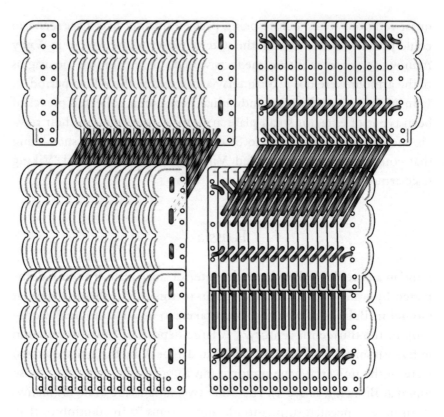

Fig. 34 Reconstruction of the 'B type' lamellar from Gomel in Belarus, thirteenth century. *Left*, outside; *right*, inside.

from Turkestan and further east into Central Asia from four or five centuries earlier.[162]

The Near East

The spread of Islam was one of the most remarkable triumphs in history. In just a couple of decades Muslims had taken control of territory from Egypt to the borders of Afghanistan. In less than a century they had added North Africa and the Iberian Peninsula. It is a doctrinal principle of Islam that it was intolerable hubris for a human to depict an animate being. This stricture was never fully observed, and from the eleventh century broke down rapidly, yet its effect was to leave scanty evidence for our subject for the early medieval period. A further complication is that while the Arabs never quite thought of themselves as 'God's Chosen People', they did feel that they, and especially the Arabic language, had been particularly blessed. This view produced a sort of informal cultural imperialism that led for centuries to cultural artefacts and practices of non-Arab Muslims being not suppressed, but often ignored in literature and art. Lamellar had never been a significant part of the military repertoire of the Arabs, and manifestly did not become so as the spread of al-Islamiyya assimilated ethnic groups who used it. Thus we are left speculating as to whether the Persians continued their Late Antique practice of protecting the man with mail and the mount with lamellar, or whether they adapted the armour to men or used it less overall. My suspicion is that the virtues of a construction as sophisticated, adaptable and protective as the lamellar shown on the horse of Khosroes (*ill. 26; fig. 20*) would soon be recognised and used to defend human lives as well those of their mounts. Certainly within a couple of centuries the universal form of hanging lamellar which may well have derived from that Sassanian type was established from Central Asia to Russia.[163] In the later tenth century a new influx of populations from lands where lamellar was common washed into Persia from the north; the Seljuk Turks. By the middle of the eleventh century they had conquered Iran and were expanding west and south. Sources from the time tell us that the Seljuks tended to be less well armoured than the troops of the nations they invaded, although precise details are not forthcoming from the early portion of the Seljuk incursion.[164] From the late twelfth century, pictorial sources begin to occur in increasing quantity and quality that embodied the Seljuks' own image of themselves.[165] These corroborate the accounts of the literature, overwhelmingly showing warriors clad in opulent textiles. The cases where helmets appear lead one to suspect that the ornate coats were often worn over mail, as was common among the Arabs. Representations of exterior small plate armour that may be lamellar do occur here and there, and they are consistent in showing hip-length jackets, very occasionally with short sleeves.[166] These pictures are all too sketchy to draw very confident conclusions as to which construction of lamellar was used by the Seljuks. The illuminations in the early thirteenth-century romance *Warqa wa Gulsha* mostly show corselets not well enough rendered to be informative in that way, but have a few instances been coloured brown, perhaps representing leather, and rather more occasions show bands of blue and yellow, probably indicating alternating rows of iron and bronze.[167]

The singular piece of relevant archaeology from the region in this period serves as much to confuse the issue as to clarify it. Among a diverse, but fragmentary, collection of military equipment found at an undisclosed location in Mesopotamia (attributed to around 1200, and now in a private collection) was a very well preserved panel of iron lamellar.[168] The plates are unique in shape – mostly virtually square with substantial dimple on the centre with eleven holes around the edges (*fig. 12.13*). The assembly method, however, is essentially the same as Cartagena and Wisby (*figs 19, 33*), with leather-edged rows bound solidly together. The finished piece has six rows which expand from thirteen to seventeen lames in a manner evidently intended to be a skirt panel. Once again, continuity of this elementary lacing structure over a span of six centuries and the length of the Mediterranean cannot reasonably be suggested, and so this, too, is probably a reinvention.

This skirt panel may have been a unique item in its own time, and hence for good reasons not precisely corroborated in other sources, but there is one strong vector of influence in the region. The adjacent great power was Constantinople, and relations between there and the nearby states were more often diplomatic than adversarial.[169] Even more so, the Christian communities, including the Crusader states, looked to the city for aid, guidance and inspiration in many areas of life, including military practice. This was reflected in art produced in the Levant, which shows various instances of exterior small plate armour – lamellar of both Byzantine and non-Byzantine forms, sometimes with scale supplementary pieces, as well as scale armour alone (*ill. 28*).[170] It is possible that the lamellar that was recycled to protect the under-equipped defenders of Wisby in the Baltic had been brought back from the Levant by Scandinavian Crusaders in this period.

The situation in Iran and Mesopotamia becomes clearer in the wake of the Mongol invasions of the early thirteenth century. The burgeoning realm of Persian manuscript painting becomes comprehensively colonised with Mongol elements, although we must always be aware that that may not reflect actual practice among the natives, especially those in lower social classes, who would be under less pressure to conform to the expectations of the new ruling elite, and would have less economic capacity to indulge any desire to imitate them.[171] So far as the manuscript tradition reflects reality, it shows a vast upsurge in the use of lamellar and other segmental armours. Manuscripts from this period and region show highly decorated laminar (banded leather) armours at least as often as they depict lamellar. Some of these are patterned in a manner which very much resembles lamellar, representing the numerous suspension laces that laminar can share with lamellar (*ill. 33*). Sources that do show lamellar are more diverse than in comparable lamellar-using cultures. Lamellar harnesses for humans include a simple tube around the chest, hip-length jackets, hip-length jackets with thigh-flaps, and integral coats falling to well beyond the knee. All forms were fitted with some sort of upper-arm defence. The simplest is a modest flap that covers just the outside of the arm to the lower biceps. Some are larger pieces, shaped with a point to fall beyond the rear of the elbow and fastened on the inside of the arm. More generally, sleeves are a full tube into the crook of the elbow or a little beyond. The sleeve structure seems to correlate quite precisely with the lamellar fabric employed. Virtually all the lamellar shown on men is distinctly banded. (Indeed, the non-banded fabrics may all actually be scale armour: *ill. 34, far right*.) None of the pictures show any fine detail on plates or bands that would clarify what specific constructions are employed, but several possibilities are plausible. The basic chest-tube-with-flap-sleeve or short jacket could be viably constructed in a simple solid-laced form similar to Cartagena/Mesopotamia/Wisby examples (*figs 19, 33*). Some do show curved edges on the lames, much like Wisby. When made of fine lames with substantial laces, the universal hanging form, which is certainly in very wide use, could appear to have a band at the top of a row as the laces blur into one another (*fig. 28*). There seem to be no well-preserved surviving examples to confirm it, but the universal hanging form might well be made with a strip of leather behind the tops of the lames and projecting upward to protect the laces. Another banded fabric which shows few surface features and which might well have been in use, is Gomel type C (*fig. 32*). Manifestly, one fabric known on the western edge of Central Asia for centuries and found at Gomel (type B: *fig. 34*) was still in use. A form of it may appear on men (*ill. 34, far right?*), but more definitely it is depicted very well on horse armours in the same *Shirazi Shahnama* manuscript (*ill. 35, particularly on the right*). The varying orientation of the rows of the rump is corroborated in surviving Central Asian lamellar horse armours from later times. It is also striking that the frontal area of this barding shows exactly the same structure as that of Khosroes II from Taq-i-Bustan 700 years earlier – the lamellar on the chest hangs in the normal orientation, while that on the throat is inverted (*ill. 26*).

The survival of lamellar in Iran through the fourteenth and into the fifteenth centuries was the swansong for this form of armour west of the Ural line. From the fifteenth century it was rapidly supplanted by larger plate armours, such as the *char-aina* (mirror armour) harnesses, and composite mail and plates arrangements, in parallel with the practices of the Ottoman Turks.

CONCLUSION

The history of exterior small plate armour is a testament to the diversity and persistence of human ingenuity. The challenge of contriving protection for the complex, flexible and dynamic structure that is the human body demanded solutions that were equally dynamic and adaptable. The availability of materials and processes further complicated this considerable challenge. Time after time, exterior small plate armour was a solution that armourers turned to and returned to, even when other methods had been tried with some success. The variability, flexibility and adaptability of scale and lamellar, and their capacity to be made from so many different materials, gave them a recurrent utility that outlasted that of other forms of armour.

The way in which so many variants arose in so many different locations and times points to some important lessons. Technological innovation is not a singular or linear process. Confronted with a similar range of resources and desired outcomes, people in different locations and situations will often devise remarkably similar solutions to a problem but with local specificities. The diversity that can be seen in lamellar constructions is clear evidence of this, although the same is doubtless true of scale armour, but would be less visible owing to the more limited range of possible scale structures.

What is more visible with scale armour is the way it has an afterlife. Art, in imitating life, may persist to inspire its own imitation in life, or to inspire a new round of invention, long after the practices that had been recorded in the art had ceased to be followed.

A caution lies in the observation that, however effective or promising a solution, it still may not endure and spread beyond the social context of its devising in a living form. The direction of change (especially technological change) is not always 'progress'. The forces which drive it, divert it or block it should be a matter for serious contemplation just as much today, in our globalised present, as in relation to history.

NOTES

1   Bengt Thordeman, *Armour from the Battle of Wisby, 1361* (Stockholm: Alqvist
    and Wiskell, 1938), p. 276. This pattern of origin and spread is acknowledged
    by Hiroshi Kajiwara: 'On lamellae: Lamellar armor from a Eurasian
    viewpoint', *Tohoku Fukushi University Serizawa Keisuke Art and Craft Museum
    Annual Report*, vol. 1, 2009, p. 57.

2   A.F. May, *Der Schmuck aus jungpaläololithischen Bestattungen in Frankreich und
    Ligurien* (Jewellery from early Palaeolithic burials in France and Liguria)
    (Berne: Fritz Marti, 1962), illustrations on p. 71.

3   See note 2.

4   See, for example, David Nicolle, *Medieval Warfare Sourcebook*, illustration on
    p. 137, which is typical of practices around the Byzantine periphery. Contrast
    that with the illustration on p. 69, where what Nicole identifies as stylised
    mail could just as easily be scale.

5   Once again, David Nicolle's work exemplifies how ideas might evolve. In
    Medieval Warfare Sourcebook (p. 91) he identifies as lamellar a picture showing
    an armour with no characteristics other than horizontal banding, while later
    in *Companion to Medieval Arms and Armour* he discusses a leather banded
    (or, as he calls it, 'hooped') armour which would produce an identical
    appearance: 'Jawshan, Cuirie and Coats-of-plates: An Alternative Line of
    Development for Hardened Leather Armour' pp. 179–221.

6   While I cordially salute Mamuka Tsurtsumia for bringing the Georgian
    evidence for external small plate armours (and Slavic scholarship) into the
    English-speaking realm, he also falls into the pictorial literalism trap in
    respect of some of those sources. 'The evolution of splint armour in Georgia
    and Byzantion, lamellar and scale armour in the 10th–12th centuries',
    BYZANTINA ΣΥΜΜΕΙΚΤΑ, 21, 2011, pp. 65–99.

7   Once again, this dating issue is one which Mamuka Tsurtsumia does not
    take sufficiently into consideration in his attempt to claim credit for banded
    lamellar for his homeland.

8   There are still those who reject practical experimentation and experience
    as inputs to scholarship. Discounting the dying breed of old-fashioned

academics who simply dismiss such things as irrelevant or inimical to scholarship, there are some potentially valid points to be considered. Rafaele D'Amato, who has written a number of books on ancient and medieval military equipment, asserts that modern manufacturers cannot match the skills of ancient and medieval craftsmen who spent their lives working within a living craft tradition which doubtless included techniques handed down from master to apprentice and never committed to any record which might have come down to us (personal communication). There is some justice in this view, but only in limited areas, such as particular aspects of high-quality metalworking. In other areas modern artisans can achieve equivalent results, albeit more slowly and less easily. The construction of external small plate armours is a technology which requires no such sophisticated input, and so is very amenable to effective reconstruction.

9   Timothy Dawson, 'Banded lamellar – a solution', *Varangian Voice*, no. 23, August 1992, p. 16. Heath's version of lamellar unfortunately remains enshrined as canonical for many historical recreationists. Ian Heath, *Byzantine Armies: 886–1118* (Oxford: Osprey, 1980), p. 8.

10 See Tsurtsumia (p. 65) for a discussion of this in relation to the eastern European scholarship. A notable case of this confusion is to be found in J. Kim Siddorn, *Viking Weapons and Warfare* (Stroud, UK: Tempus, 2000). On p. 59f the author says there is no evidence for the use of lamellar among Vikings, but goes on to declare that 'a very thin case can be made for the use of scale by returning members of the Varangian Guard from Constantinople'. He accompanies this statement with figure 24 which shows a lamellar corselet clearly based upon Byzantine pictures, but which is labelled 'Scale, note the overlap is upward'. One can only speculate on what Siddorn thinks of as being lamellar.

11 Doubtless there will be some people who will chide me for an omission in this volume – broad-ring armour: the type composed of rings laced or stitched to a leather garment. The persistence of that nineteenth-century invention in the popular imagination is perversely admirable! I will admit that as a young and ignorant re-enactor I made such an armour myself, although it only took the first thrust to arrive painfully at my chest without any metal contact to tell me that there was something fundamentally wrong with the concept.

12 Tsurtsumia, p. 67.

13 The most familiar examples of such misrendered lamellar can be seen in the illuminated Madrid manuscript of the *Chronicle* of John Skylitzes on ff. 126 (a particularly clumsy example), 135, 140v (again, extremely garbled), 153v, 154v and 212v. The *Madrid Skylitzes* manuscript was illustrated in Sicily around the middle of the twelfth century, and while some of the illustrators were at least very familiar with Byzantine iconography and almost certainly working from earlier Byzantine pictures, and may even have seen some lamellar, others were manifestly not so familiar and did not understand what they were meant to be

representing. The most recent comprehensive study of the manuscript is Vasiliki Tsamakda, *The Illustrated Chronicle of the Ioannis Skylitzes in Madrid* (Leiden: Brill, 2002). Some of the Georgian pictures show the same sort of garbled representation. See Tsurtsumia (figs 12, 15, and 26) for Georgian examples.

14 See note 11.

15 *Stuttgart Psalter*, f. 70v.

16 http://www.culture.gouv.fr/fr/arcnat/charavines/en/legende/190.htm for a picture of the warrior reconstruction. http://www.culture.gouv.fr/fr/arcnat/charavines/en/legende/194.htm shows a plate.

17 See David Nicolle's article on banded armour made of treated leather referred to in note 5. See also Arkadiusz Michalak, 'Was leather armour used on Polish lands in the Medieval period?' for a discussion of the spread of evidence for leather armour in Antiquity and the Middle Ages.

18 A published excursion in this field is T. Dawson, 'The Walpurgis Fechtbuch: an inheritance of Constantinople?', *Arms and Armour*, Royal Armouries Museum, 2009.

19 Tests originally detailed in T. Dawson, '*Kremasmata, Kabbadion, Klivanion*: Some aspects of middle Byzantine military equipment reconsidered', *Byzantine and Modern Greek Studies*, 22, 1998, p. 45.

20 Rafaele D'Amato, *Arms and Armour of the Imperial Roman Soldier: from Marius to Commodus, 112 BC–AD 192* (London: Frontline Books, 2009), p. 102.

21 A very valuable recent contribution from someone with the requisite linguistic knowledge is Manouchehr Moshtagh Khorasani, 'Linguistic terms describing different types of armour in Persian manuscripts', *Gladius*, XXXI, 2011, pp. 149–188. Note especially the discussion of *jōšan*, which deconstructs its use in English publications of recent years.

22 Nineteenth- and early twentieth-century archaeology was notoriously obsessed with the Classical world. It was not unusual for medieval material to be treated as rubbish to be removed on the way down to Classical material, or for suitable medieval finds to be designated as Antique in order to enhance the productivity of a site. Even when a more rigorous approach prevailed, stratigraphy techniques were primitive, and there were no methods of scientific dating. Hence, the dates attributed to all archaeological material from that era must be treated with caution.

23 M. Von Groller, 'Römische Waffen', *Der Römische Limes in Österreich*, 2, 1901, pp. 85–132.

24 Michael Gorelik, *Battle of Kulikov 1380: Russian Troops and the Golden Horde*, 1983.

25 Rivka Gonen, *Weapons of the Ancient World* (London: Cassell, 1975), p. 83.

26 There is a suggestion that bone or ivory scales of type 1 found at Pompeii were fastened with wire (D'Amato, p. 144). This suggestion appears to go back to a mid-nineteenth-century publication and should be discounted for practical reasons. Like riveting, wire-tying to the base garment is likely to cause damage to it, and in this case is also likely to damage the scales themselves.

27 James K. Hoffmeier. 'Military', *The Oxford Encyclopaedia of Ancient Egypt*, vol II, p. 410.

28 A.E. Negin, 'Sarmatian Cataphracts as prototypes for Roman *equites cataphractarii*', *Journal of Roman Military Equipment Studies*, 9, 1998, plate 5.3.

29 Negin, plate 5.5.

30 Book 7, section 61.

31 Book 9, section 22.

32 This term is sometimes applied to a hybrid armour in which scales are mounted upon mail, but I agree with Wijnhoven that this is incorrect. See M.A. Wijnhoven, '*Lorica Hamata Squamataque*: a study of Roman hybrid armour', *Journal of the Mail Research Society*, 2009, vol. 2, no. 1, pp. 3–29. See also D'Amato, p. 142.

33 ROM, acc. no. 930.77.19. See Robinson (1975, p. 153) for pictures of front and back. The dubious, and possibly modern, elements are the standing collar, epaulettes and armhole edgings.

34 D'Amato, p. 141.

35 Robinson, *Armour of Imperial Rome*, p. 156.

36 C. Howard-Davis, *The Carlisle Millennium Project*, vol. 2. p. 689.

37 For example, the *Vatican Virgil*: Vat. Lat. 3867, f. 188v, late fifth century, shows thigh-length *loricae squamatae* with elbow-length sleeves. The precision of the rendering and resemblance to other pictures, both earlier and later, negates Nicolle's conclusion that these armours are 'probably mail' (*Medieval Warfare Sourcebook*, p. 21).

38 Volume 2, no. 1 of *The Journal of the Mail Research Society* is entirely devoted to this armour, with three very detailed articles. See also Peter Price, 'An interesting find of Lorica Plumata from the Roman fortress of Usk', in M.C. Bishop (ed.), *Roman Military Equipment* (Department of Ancient History, University of Sheffield, 1983), pp. 12–13.

39 M.A. Wijnhoven, '*Lorica Hamata Squamataque*', p. 28.

40 J. Curtis (ed.), Mesopotamia and Iran in the Parthian and Sassanian Periods, p. 42.

41 V.N. Pilipko, 'Arms and armours from Old Nisa', p. 264 and fig. 13.

42 For a survey of the state of the scholarship see Grotowski, p. 126, n. 5.

43 Perì Stratêgías 27.17: *Dennis, Three Treatises*, p. 86.

44 *Stratêgikon*, I.2 and VII.15: Dennis (ed.), pp. 80 and 258/Dennis (trans.), 14 and 76.

45 Haldon also believes so: *Early Byzantine Arms and Armour*, p. 69.

46 *Stratêgikon*, I.2: Dennis (ed.) p. 78/Dennis (trans.) 12. Dennis' English translation tends to give the impression that the hood was part of the *zava*, but X.1 (Dennis (ed.), p. 338/Dennis (trans.), p. 106) shows them to be separate by suggesting that they should be shared with men lacking armour.

47 Despite the fact that the Greek is beyond doubt, and later manuals which preserved that portion of the *Stratêgikon*'s advice saw no reason to alter it.

48 Rylands Coptic S. 33: Christopher Walter, *The Warrior Saints in Byzantine Art and Tradition* (Aldershot, UK: Ashgate, 2003), p. 56. Walter suggests the picture might be from as late as the ninth century (p. xiii) but no date has been plausibly established (p. 186).

49 Leo, *Taktika*, Ch. 5, §3: Dennis (ed. & trans.), p. 72. Dennis' translation (p. 72) suggests that single shirts might combine mail with the other material, but the Greek can more plausibly be interpreted as meaning that, if possible, all of the armour should be mail, but if not, some may be of other materials.

50 St George, ms. 587, Dionysiou Monastery, Mount Athos, f. 151v (Grotowski, fig. 46c). A twelfth-century soapstone icon of Sts George and Theodore in the State Historical Museum, Moscow (Grotowski, fig. 40). While not precisely attested in archaeology, a fresco in the Church of St Barbara (Tatali Kilese), Soğanli Valley, Kappadokhia from around 1000 shows rectilinear scales with double bosses comparable to Georgian icons.

51 Soldiers at the Passion, fresco, *c.*1250, Church of Vlakhernai, Arta, Greece; St George, fresco *c.*1300, Church of St John Khrysostom, Geraki, Greece; Soldiers at the Passion, fresco, 1311, Church of Hodigêtria, Spilies, Euboia, Greece; Military saint, fresco 1314/15, Church of Christ the Saviour, Veroia, Greece; St Prokopios, fresco, 1315/20, Church of the Holy Saviour in Khora, Istanbul; St George, fresco 1334/5, Dečani Monastery, Kosovo. Babuine figs IX.7, 17, 21, 27, 29 respectively.

52 Many also have a tenuous understanding of arms and armour. For example, in *Armies of the Caliphs*, Hugh Kennedy describes scale armour construction while calling it lamellar (p. 168). Elsewhere he adds another layer of confusion to David Nicolle's work by interpreting a sketch of ankle-length armour as 'lamellar leggings' (p. 169).

53 Thordeman, p. 246. no. 10.

54 Dezso Csallány, *A Kunszentmártoni Avarkori Ötvössír (Goldschmiedegrab aus der Avarenzeit von Kunszentmárton (Ungarn))* (A Goldsmith's Grave of the Avar Period from Kunszentmárton (Hungary)) (Szentes, 1933), p. 14.

55 Peter Paulsen, *Alamannische Adelsgraber von Niederstotzingen* (An Allemannic Noble Grave from Niederstotzingen) (Stuttgart: Verlag-Müller & Gräff, 1967), p. 126.

56 Simon Coupland, 'Carolingian arms and armour in the ninth century', *Viator: Medieval and Renaissance Studies*, 21, 1990, p. 41.

57 Bernard S. Bachrach, *Early Carolingian Warfare: Prelude to Empire* (Philadelphia: University of Pennsylvania Press, 2001).

58 *Stuttgart Psalter*, ff. 42v., 66v., 71v.

59 *Stuttgart Psalter*, ff. 15r, 21r, 31r, 70r, 78v, 89r, 95r.

60 *Stuttgart Psalter*, ff. 21v. The Psalter has been outstandingly digitised at http://digital.wlb-stuttgart.de/purl/bsz307047059.

61 *Stuttgart Psalter*, ff. 44v, 95r, 107v, 137v, 143r, 146v, 150v, 153r.

62 For example, a steatite icon of saints. Theodore Stratelatês, George and

Demetrios; Hermitage Museum, St Petersburg, eleventh to twelfth centuries (right figure), and numerous others.

63 *Stuttgart Psalter*, f. 5v.

64 *Stuttgart Psalter*, f. 88r.

65 *Stuttgart Psalter*, f. 70v: possibly garbled lamellar (orthogonal squares). f. 130r: seemingly, a muscled cuirass.

66 *Stuttgart Psalter*, f. 158v.

67 A.J. Grant (ed. & trans.), *Early Lives of Charlemagne by Eginhard and the Monk of St Gall* (London: Chatto & Windus, 1926), p. 146.

68 Nikêforos Fôkas, *Composition on Warfare*, III.4. See Timothy Dawson, 'Suntagma Hoplôn: the equipment of regular Byzantine troops, *c.*950–*c.*1204', in D. Nicolle (ed.), *Companion to Medieval Arms and Armour* (London: Boydell & Brewer, 2002), p. 85 etc.

69 *Stuttgart Psalter*, f. 311r.

70 FGA, Washington, 32–18, f. 310: Nicolle, *Sourcebook*, II, p. 137.

71 St George of Chikhareshi (Tsurtsumia, fig. 6), St Procopius, Georgia National Manuscripts Centre, ms A648, p. 60r (Tsurtsumia, fig. 8), St Theodore, Processional cross from Sakdari, and several other examples.

72 See Nicolle, *Sourcebook*, vol. 2, p. 115, for a picture of these scales mounted.

73 Steatite icon of Saints George and Theodore, Constantinople? Twelfth century, State Historical Museum, Moscow; after Lazarev. See also Evans and Wixom, *Glory of Byzantion*, no. 80.

74 A standard work on this subject remains Ralph-Johannes Lillie, *Byzantion and the Crusader States* (Oxford: Clarendon Press, 1993).

75 British Library, ms. Or. 7170, 'Christ before Pilate', f. 145r.

76 These pictures have frequently been reproduced in full colour in Byzantine and Crusader art books. For Sergios and Bakkhos in monochrome, see Dawson, *Byzantine Cavalryman*, p. 56.

77 Bashford Dean's identification of three pieces of metal found in the Crusader castle of Montfort and now in the Metropolitan Museum as armour scales manifestly owes more to his perception that the Metropolitan Museum's collection had an unconscionable lacuna in its lack of armour from that period than to any reasonable assessment of the shapeless and featureless scraps of iron. See Dean, 'The exploration of a Crusaders' fortress (Montfort) in Palestine,' pp. 36–37 and fig. 53 for the plates, and p. 5 for his lament about the museum's lack.

78 A relief of the twelfth century, Art Museum, Seattle, inv. 54.29 (one warrior with sleeves). An Atruqid (Northern Mesopotamia) coin of 1199–1200: Hillenbrand, *Islamic Art and Architecture*, p. 133. Stone relief, thirteenth century, Museum of Turkish and Islamic Art, Istanbul (both warriors with sleeves): Hattstein and Delius (eds), *Islamic Art and Architecture*, p. 353.

79 Nowadays erroneously called 'Byzantines'. The continued use of 'Roman' as the designation for them and their state, both by them and by other nations around them, is the basis for the new kingdom created by the Seljuks in

Anatolia being called the 'Sultanate of Rum'.

80   Michael Gorelik, 'Oriental armour of the Near and Middle East …', p. 54, nos 78–81.

81   Scales were found at Tuva: Alan Williams, *The Sword and the Crucible*, p. 33.

82   Bibliotheque Royale of Albert lst, ms. 9245, f. 245r. Reproduced in Christopher Gravett, *Medieval German Armies*, p. 46.

83   Dobra, Durdik and Wagner, *Medieval Costume, Armour and Weapons*, plates 6.1, 13.1 & 2, and 15.

84   Krumlov ms. 38f. (gorget and skirt) and 58f. (skirt only): Dobra, Durdik and Wagner, *Medieval Costume, Armour and Weapons*, plates 17 and 19 respectively.

85   At the time of writing, a number of websites offer excellent views of all the illumination of the *Cantigas de Santa Maria*, such as http://warfare.totalh. net/Cantiga/Cantigas_de_Santa_Maria.htm.

86   See Nicole, *Medieval Warfare Sourcebook*, vol. II, p. 166 for a close-up photograph.

87   Ada Brun de Hofmeyer, *Arms and Armour in Spain, A Short Survey*, vol. II, p. 119.

88   A soldier on the retable of Church of Sang d'Alcover, Tarragona, Brun de Hofmeyer, *Arms and Armour in Spain, A Short Survey, vol II*, p, 227, fig. 84; soldiers in the cloisters of the Cathedral of Pamplona, Brun de Hofmeyer, *Arms and Armour in Spain, A Short Survey, vol. II*, p. 230, fig. 86.

89   The most notorious and overused example is the illuminated manuscript of the *Chronicle* of John Skylitzes, now in the National Library, Madrid. The text may derive from Constantinople, but the illustrations were executed in Sicily by people who had never been to the City, and who had obviously never actually seen a Byzantine soldier wearing lamellar. See Nigel G. Wilson, 'The Madrid Skylitzes', *Scrittura e Civilita*, 2, 1978, pp. 209–219 and Vasiliki Tsamakda, *The Illustrated Chronicle of the Ioannis Skylitzes in Madrid*.

90   Shown in Nicolle, *Medieval Warfare Sourcebook*, vol. I, p. 244.

91   Massacre of the Innocents, relief in Linköping Cathedral, late thirteenth century: Nicolle, *Sourcebook I*, p. 137. The style is also illustrated in the Low Countries into the fourteenth century: H.M. Zijlstra-Zweens, *Of His Array Telle I No Lenger Tale: Aspects of Costume, Arms and Armour in Western Europe, 1200–1400* (Amsterdam: Rodopi, 1988), p. 89.

92   Illustration 13: RAM inv. no. III.4323. Also RAM III.1339.

93   See Stuart W. Pyhrr, *Heroic Armor of the Italian Renaissance*, pp. 296–301 for an array of examples.

94   Hermitage; no inventory record available.

95   Wallace Collection, A284, *c.* 1620. Preserves its original form, and may retain its original leather. RAM II.192 is a plate harness complete in its original components, possibly made in Brescia, for Count Annabile Capodistra in around 1620. The *culet* of this armour is identical to that in the Wallace Collection, with one exception. It was restored in the nineteenth century as two panels divided in the centre. It is interesting to note that the

restoration may well have been done so that the armour could be worn at the Eglinton Tournament in 1839. RAM III.698 has been remounted in the same overall shape as Wallace A284, but with the scales inverted and the flanged rectangular plates along the top loose at their bottoms. The plates in the top row had two rivets at their lower edge which originally secured them to the leather base under the top row of true scales. A scale *culet* auctioned by Christies in July 2000 had scales overlapping downward, but this can also be explained by the fact that the entire piece had been remounted (http://www.christies.com/lotfinder/LotDetailsPrintable. aspx?intObjectID=1841666). The same piece was more recently resold by Fagan Arms, whose website has better images (and a remarkably different description): http://www.faganarms.com/agothicbreastplatespanishoritalian- late15thcentury-1500-3.aspx?MMP=101O18U8QAU. Christies auctioned another scaled *culet* in June 1979, but no details are available.

96 The account of the find is in Hugh C. Rogers and Donald J. LaRocca, 'A New World find of European scale armor', *Gladius*, vol. XIX, 1999, pp. 221–230.

97 Metropolitan Museum, acc. no. 1998.366.1–6.

98 Rogers and LaRocca (pp. 229–30) for the various possibilities; LaRocca, *Arms and Armor: Notable Acquisitions, 1991–2002* (New York: Metropolitan Museum of Art, 2001), p. 34 for the singular theory.

99 I am very much indebted to Peter Bleed, previously of the University of Nebraska–Lincoln, for information regarding the John Gregory Bourke armour.

100 Personal communication from Peter Bleed.

101 Metropolitan Museum, acc. no. 19.49.16. Bashford Dean, *Helmets and Body Armor in Modern Warfare* (New Haven, CT: Yale University Press, 1920), pp. 59–60, fig. 16.

102 Information kindly provided by Donald LaRocca, Metropolitan Museum Curator of Armour.

103 Metropolitan Museum, acc. no. 11.215.452.

104 Terrence Wise, *Ancient Armies of the Middle East* (Oxford: Osprey, 1987), p. 20. Cited in Hilary & John Travis, *Roman Body Armour* (Stroud, UK: Amberley Publishing, 2012), p. 97.

105 Thordeman, fig. 232.60–61. Thordeman states that these are also in the Metropolitan Museum. The smaller of these may be the fragmentary item (accession number: 34.1.73a–c).

106 Metropolitan Museum, acc. no. 61.100.53.

107 Thordeman, pp. 276–78; Robinson, *Oriental Armour*, pp. 7–8.

108 BM inv. no. WA 118907.

109 BM inv. no. WA 124556.

110 Thordeman, p. 277.

111 Gjerstad *et al.*, *SCE*, vol. IV, part 2, p. 133; Thordeman, p. 273.

112 *SCE*, vol. II, pl. CLXXII.

113 Those doing the reconstruction acknowledge that it was entirely conjectural, and explain that they could not overlap the scales in the way they hypothesised because many of the holes were corroded shut (*SCE*, vol. II, p. 538).

114 Thordeman, p. 273.

115 Peter Connolly, *Greece and Rome at War* (London: Greenhill Books, 1998), p. 57.

116 British Museum, acc. no. GR1859:3-1:24. Labelled 'Probably north-eastern Etruria *c.*400–350 BCE'.

117 It is especially conspicuous on a third-century BCE figurine in the Walters Gallery, Baltimore (inv. no. 54.1074).

118 A fragmentary statue of a man (possibly a local king); Michal Gawlikowski, 'The Statues of the Sanctuary of Allat in Palmyra', p. 403, fig. 4. Stone relief of three gods, first century, Yale University Art Gallery. Limestone relief of the god Shadrafa, 55 CE, British Museum, acc. no. ME 125206. Relief of the gods Baal, Yarhibal and Aglibal, first century, National Museum of Syria.

119 Wiesehöfer, *Ancient Persia*, pl. XX.

120 Simon James, *The Excavations at Dura-Europos Conducted by Yale University and the French Academy of Inscriptions and Letters 1928–37* (London: British Museum Press, 2004), p. 123.

121 Metropolitan Museum acc. no. 2001.268, Tibet, fifteenth to seventeenth centuries. RAM acc. no. XXVIA.106, China, eighteenth century.

122 *Stratêgikon* XI.1 'Ὁπλίζεαι δὲ ζάβαις καὶ λωρίκοις' (ed. Dennis, trans. Gallimscheg, p. 354). Nicolle, in his *Sourcebook* (p. 38) erroneously attributes lamellar to the late Sassanians by placing his own interpretation on Dennis's already loose English translation of the remark on p. 114, although he acknowledges a reservation about this shortly afterwards.

123 See the discussion in Part 1.

124 The pieces are now in the Metropolitan Museum, which says no more than 'Sassanian period, C3rd–7th'. Coin finds at Qasr-i-Abu Nasr give a period of 500–750 CE: Donald S. Whitcomb, 'Before the roses and nightingales: excavations at Qasr-i Abu Nasr, Old Shiraz' (New York: Metropolitan Museum of Art, 1985), p. 21. The original excavations were done in the early 1930s by the old-style tomb-raiders who disregarded anything not made of precious metal or otherwise highly artistic. Whitcomb came along much later and prepared this book from Metropolitan Museum records. For the proportion of metals see p. 169. The only indication of how the bronze plates were distributed is 'thirteen iron scales were alternated with one made of bronze'; not, as a number of popular publications have had it, alternating rows of iron and bronze.

125 V. Yu. Vdovin and V. P. Nikonorov, 'Fragments of armour of the late Sassanian period from Togolok-Depe', *Journal of the Turkmen SSR Academy of Sciences, Humanities Series*, no. 4, 1991, pp. 77–79.

126 Peter Paulsen, *Alamannische Adelsgraber von Niederstotzingen* (Stuttgart:

Verlag-Muller & Graff, 1967).

127 Renate Pirling, *Das Romisch-Fränkische Gräberfeld von Krefeld-Gellep,*
1964–1965 (The Romano-Frankish Cemetery of Krefeld-Gellep) (Berlin:
Gebr. Mann Verlag, 1979), vol. I, pp. III–15.

128 Polonia Bitenc and Timotej Knific, (eds), *Od Rimljanov do Slovanov. Predmeti*
(Ljubljana: Slovenian National Museum, 2001), p. 72, cat. no. 226 and 74,
cat. no. 236, 238.

129 Paulsen, p.126, fig. 62, nos 14–17.

130 Paulsen, plate 22.

131 Pirling's lacing diagram on p. 113 is thoroughly muddled.

132 Paulsen, pp. 134, 136.

133 See Damien Glad, 'The empire's influence on barbarian elites from the
Pontus to the Rhine (fifth to seventh centuries): a case study of lamellar
weapons and segmental helmet' for a survey.

134 For examples: Metropolitan Museum acc. no. 1999.158, a Mongolian or
Tibetan helm of the thirteenth to fifteenth centuries; and several more
recent examples in the Royal Armouries Museum.

135 Leo, *Taktika,* Ch. 6, §26, ed. & trans. Dennis, p. 96. *Syllogê Taktikôn* Ch. 38, §4
and §7 and Ch. 39, §1 and §6 similarly say iron or horn. It should be noted
that the term used throughout these volumes is *sidêros* (σίδηρος), and while
khalkos (χαλκός) might be used in a general sense for various metals, *sidêros* is
always specific.

136 Leo, *Taktika,* Ch. 6, §4, ed. & trans. Dennis, p. 84.

137 Leo, *Taktika,* Ch. 19, §14, ed. & trans. Dennis, p. 508.

138 Composition on Warfare, Ch. III, §4, ed. & trans. McGeer, p. 34.

139 Metropolitan Museum, inv. no. 17.190.132.

140 Tsurtsumia, p. 75f and fig. 9.

141 Mine Kiraz, Istanbul Archaeological Museum, personal correspondence,
30 November 2010.

142 Gerrard Brett, Günter Martiny and Robert B.K. Stevenson, *The Great*
Palace of the Byzantine Emperors: Being a First Report on the Excavations
Carried Out on Behalf of the Walker Trust 1935–38 (London, 1947), p. 99. The
description goes thus: 'The normal fragments were found in six regular
sizes. They varied in width from 3 to 6cm; where the whole piece was
found, the length was approximately twice the width. All were pierced
with holes for attachment; the regular arrangement was three along one
end, one on the other, and two along each side. On more than half the
examples of each size a flange along the centre was beaten out from back
to front.'

143 Atticism was a literary fashion by which authors set out to emulate what
they perceived to be the style of the canonical writers of Classical Greece.
This was done by avoiding the use of contemporary terminology, and
describing events, situations, practices and objects in ways that would have
been recognisable to ancient readers rather than contemporary ones. See

Herbert Hunger, 'On the Imitation (ΜΙΜΗΣΙΣ) of Antiquity', Dumbarton Oaks Papers, 23–24, 1969–70, pp. 15–38.

144 *Niketas Choniatês Historia*, ed. Jan-Louis Van Dieten, Vienna, 1975, 62.95 and 197.18.

145 See T. Dawson, 'Klivanion revisited: an evolutionary typology and catalogue of middle Byzantine lamellar', *Journal of Roman Military Equipment Studies*, 12/13, 2001/02, pp. 11–24 and *One Thousand Years of Lamellar Construction in the Roman World* (Armidale: Levantia Guides no. 8, 2003, 2010).

146 The *Stratêgikon* §1.2 mentions the use of Avar lances and collars (Mavrikios, p. 78/Dennis, tr. p. 12), and Avar horse armour, tunics and tents (p. 80/p. 13).

147 See Lynn Jones, *Between Islam and Byzantion: Aght'amar and the Visual Construction of Medieval Armenian Rulership* (Aldershot, UK: Ashgate, 2007), Chapter 1 for an outline of the situation in the centuries leading up to the construction of the Church of the Holy Cross.

148 Jones (see note above) hints towards this possibility in observing (p. 94) that the biblical characters shown on the exterior of the church are all famous liberators of their respective peoples. It is noteworthy that the military saints shown on the church are all clad in scale armours, appropriately harking back to Roman practice in the periods in which they are supposed to have lived.

149 Mamuka Tsurtsumia's suggestion that banded lamellar may have been invented in Georgia cannot be entertained. In addition to these draughts-manship issues, there is the unreliability of art history dating practices discussed in the Introduction.

150 Tsurtsumia, p. 80. For the date of the of the Jruchi Second Tetraevangelion, see Peter Skinner, Dimitri Tumanishvili, and Ana Shanshiashvili (eds), *The Caucasus: Georgia on the Crossroads. Cultural Exchanges across the Europe and Beyond* (Tbilisi: Georgian Arts and Culture Centre, 2011), p. 127.

151 The reconstruction proposed by the original publication and reproduced by Tsurtsumia (fig. 22) is not at all persuasive. It has two-thirds of each plate concealed, which is a gross weight and material penalty for little benefit, and their lacing system has an excessive quantity of binding laces with a scanty and poorly secured suspension lace.

152 *Stuttgart Psalter*, f. 70v. The lamellar suggestion was discussed in online fora.

153 Dawson, 'Suntagma Hoplôn', plate VII-1c.

154 Even the most peaceable agricultural community of the Middle Ages could be assumed to have arrows for hunting, and arrows and spears for defence against predators such as wolves and bears. Michel Colardelle and Éric Verdel (eds), *Les habitats du lac de Paladru (Isère) dans leur environnement. La formation d'un terroir au XIIe siècle* (Paris: Documents d'Archéologie Française 40, Éditions de la Maison des Sciences de l'Homme, 1993), pp. 217–18.

155 Nicolle, *Carolingian Cavalryman*, plate H and notes.

156 Curiously, these is no equivalent passion for 'Viking scale armour', despite there being just as much reason for that. Part of the reason is that the field is replete with confusion. An example is J. Kim Siddorn, *Viking Weapons and*

Warfare (Stroud, UK: Tempus, 2000). On p. 59f, the author says there is no evidence for the use of lamellar among Vikings, but goes on to declare that 'a very thin case can be made for the use of scale by returning members of the Varangian Guard from Constantinople'. He accompanies this statement with figure 24 which shows a lamellar corselet clearly based upon Byzantine pictures, but which is labelled 'Scale; note the overlap is upward'. One can only speculate on what Siddorn thinks of as being lamellar.

157 *Laxdaela Saga*, Chapter 63: 'Next there sat a man and looked out of the circle; he was in a plate-corselet and had a steel cap on his head, with a brim a hand's breadth wide' (trans. Muriel A.C. Press, London: J.M. Dent & Co., 1899), p. 222.

158 Thordeman, p. 400.

159 O.L. Makushnikov and Y.M. Lupinenko, 'Lamellar armour of the Eastern Slav warrior of the beginning of the 13th century (according to the materials of Gomel excavations)', *Historical-Archaeological Studies*, 18, 2003. I am grateful to Mamuka Tsurtsumia for making details of this publication available to me.

160 The reconstructions proposed by the original publication for all the Gomel forms are not at all persuasive. Their 'type a' bears no resemblance to any of the copious surviving examples of the type (for example, RAM XXVIA.18, XXVIA.122 and the sleeves of XXVIA.106 (ill. 25)). The lacing systems of the other two types have an excessive number of binding laces with scanty and poorly secured suspension laces.

161 Spiral-binding the edges allows for greater flexibility, which would more readily facilitate the installation of the internal laces, but straight-lacing is more aesthetically pleasing to modern eyes, so in my reconstruction I have used both, with the straight in the visible location. But that is merely a concession to modern taste, not anything historical.

162 Guitty Azarpay, *Sogdian Painting: The Pictorial Epic in Oriental Art* (Berkeley, CA: University of California Press, 1981), p. 106. Also in Helmut Nickel, 'The mutual influence of Europe and Asia ...', p. 112 and pl. X.22.

163 Mikhail Gorelik, 'Arms and armour in south-eastern Europe ...', p. 137, plate XI.12.10, and elsewhere.

164 John W. Birkenmeier, *The Development of the Komnenian Army, 1081–1180* (Leiden: Brill, 2002), p. 208.

165 These sources range from stone relief carvings, through large quantities of gorgeous lustre ceramics with figural decoration, to a few finely illuminated manuscripts.

166 A relief of the twelfth century, Art Museum, Seattle, inv. 54.29 (one warrior with sleeves). An Atruqid (Northern Mesopotamia) coin of 1199–1200: Hillenbrand, *Islamic Art and Architecture*, p. 133. Stone relief, thirteenth century, Museum of Turkish and Islamic Art, Istanbul (both warriors with sleeves): Hattstein and Delius (eds), *Islamic Art and Architecture*, p. 353. Shown in various places in the illuminated romance of

Warqa wa Gulsha.

167 *Warqa wa Gulsha* f.22/21a, a brown cuirass; f. 20, f. 24/23b and other alternating colours.

168 David Nicolle, *Arms and Armour of the Crusading Era*, vol. 2, p. 180/no. 423.

169 See various entries in the *Book of Gifts and Rarities*, for an impression of high-level contacts between Constantinople and Muslim rulers.

170 British Library, ms. Or. 7170, 'Betrayal of Jesus', f. 143v.

171 One reason to be sceptical of the manuscripts is the extensive suite of copies of the *World History* of Rashid ad-Din, produced in Tabriz, and some manuscripts of the *Shahnama* of Firdawsi, which routinely show banded armours overlapping downward with a large step, even on the chest. The practical reasons for doubting such a construction are set out in the section on the protective functionality of the armours in the Introduction. Hence, one must suspect that those artists, at least, were not familiar with lamellar. Other sources are less doubtful.

KEY TO THE SCALES
AND LAMES
COLLECTIONS

Figure 1: Scales from archaeology, location and period:
Type 1: 1, 2, 3 – Memphis, Egypt, C14th BCE; 4 – Königshofen, Germany; 5, 6 – Vorobyi Viatka Province, Russia; 7 – Tiffliskaya Stanitsa, Cuban, Russia; 8 – Yourovka, Province of Kiev; 9 – Italy (Brescia?), early C17th (largest size); 10, 11 – Nebraska, USA, early C19th.
Type 2: 1, 2 – Memphis, Egypt, C14th BCE; 3 – Greatchesters, England, C3rd, 4, 5 – Carnuntum, Austria; 6 – Mainz-Wissenau, Germany; 7 – Tenginskaya, Cuban, Russia; 8 – Sisak, Croatia; 9 – Russia, C13–14th.
Type 3: 1 – Tchiguirin, Province of Kiev; 2, 3 – Kertch, Ukraine, C5th; 4 – Cuban, Russia; 5 – Birka, Sweden, C10th.
Type 4: 1 – Chester, England; 2 – Newstead, England; 3 – Camp Hill, Somerset, England; 4, 5 – Carlisle, Scotland, early C2nd; 6 – Egypt; 7 – Vidovgrad, Russia; 8, 9, 10 – Sisak, Croatia; 11 – Kunszentmárton, Hungary, C6th; 12 – Kirchheim/ Reis, Germany; 13 – Dilingen, Germany; 14, 15 – Kertch, Ukraine, C5th; 16 – Birka, Sweden, C10th; 17 – Tiffliskaya Stanitsa, Cuban, Russia.
Type 5: 1, 2 – Cambridge, England; 3, 4 – Carlisle, Scotland, early C2nd; 5 – Kastell Aalen, Germany; 6, 7 – Sotin, Croatia; 8, 9, 10 – Carnuntum, Austria.

Figure 12: Lames from archaeology, location and period:
1 – Malqata, Egypt, C14th BCE; 2 – Hasanlu, Iran, c. C9th BCE; 3 – Idalion, Cyprus, C5th BCE; 4 – Amathus, Cyprus, C5th BCE; 5 – Wisby, C5–6th?; 6 – Cartagena, Spain, C6th; 7 – Qasr-i-abu Nasr, Iran, C6th; 8 – Krefeld-Gellep, Germany, c. 540; 9 – Kertch, Ukraine, C5th; 10 – Birka, Sweden, C10th; 11 – Turfan, Turkestan, C10th–14th; 12 – Constantinople, late C12th (largest size); Mesopotamia, C12th–13th.

BIBLIOGRAPHY

Anonymous, *Book of Gifts and Rarities*, trans. Ghâda al-Hijjâwî al-Qaddûmî
(Cambridge, MA: Harvard University Press, 1996).

Anonymous, *Laxdaela Saga*, trans. Muriel A.C. Press (London: J.M. Dent & Co.,
1899)

Andersson, T.M., *The Growth of the Medieval Icelandic Sagas, 1180–1280* (Ithaca, NY:
Cornell University Press, 2006).

Azarpay, G., *Sogdian Painting: The Pictorial Epic in Oriental Art* (Berkeley, CA:
University of California Press, 1981).

Bachrach, B.S., *Early Carolingian Warfare: Prelude to Empire* (Philadelphia, PA:
University of Pennsylvania Press, 2001).

Beridze, V.V., *The Treasures of Georgia* (London: Century Publishing, 1984).

Birkenmeier, J.W., *The Development of the Komnenian Army, 1081–1180* (Leiden:
Brill, 2002).

Bitenc, P. and Knific, T. (eds), *Od Rimljanov do Slovanov. Predmeti* (Ljubljana:
Slovenian National Museum, 2001).

Brett, G., Martiny, G. and Stevenson, R.B.K., *The Great Palace of the Byzantine
Emperors: Being a First Report on the Excavations carried out on behalf of the Walker
Trust 1935–38* (London: Publisher, 1947).

Brun de Hoffmeyer, A., *Arms and Armour in Spain: A Short Survey*, Vol. I (Madrid,
1971).

Brun de Hoffmeyer, A., *Arms and Armour in Spain: A Short Survey*, Vol. II (Madrid,
1982).

Bugarski, I, 'A contribution to the study of lamellar armours', *Starinar*, 2005, 161–79.

Choniatês, Niketas, *Historia*, ed. Jan-Louis Van Dieten (Vienna, 1975).

Colardelle M. and Verdel, É. (eds), *Les habitats du lac de Paladru (Isère) dans leur
environnement. La formation d'un terroir au XIIe siècle*, Documents d'Archéologie
Française 40 (Paris: Éditions de la Maison des Sciences de l'Homme, 1993).

Colledge, M.A.R., *Parthian Art* (London: Elek, 1977).

Connolly, P., *Greece and Rome at War* (London: Greenhill Books, 1998).

Coupland, S., 'Carolingian arms and armour in the ninth century', *Viator:
Medieval and Renaissance Studies*, vol. 21, 1990, pp. 29–50.

Cowan, R., *Imperial Roman Legionary: AD 161–284* (Oxford: Osprey, 2003).

Csallány, D., A *Kunszentmártoni Avarkori Ötvössír (Goldschmiedegrab aus der Avarenzeit von Kunszentmárton (Ungarn))*, (Szentes 1933).

Curtis, J. (ed.), *Mesopotamia and Iran in the Parthian and Sassanian periods: rejection and revival, c.238 BC–AD 642. Proceedings of a seminar in memory of Vladimir G. Lukonin* (London: British Museum Press, 2000).

D'Amato, R., *Arms and Armour of the Imperial Roman Soldier: from Marius to Commodus, 112 BC–AD 192* (London: Frontline Books, 2009).

Dawson, T., 'Banded lamellar – a solution', *Varangian Voice*, no. 23, August 1992.

Dawson, T., 'Kremasmata, Kabbadion, Klibanion: Some aspects of middle Byzantine military equipment reconsidered', *Byzantine and Modern Greek Studies*, 22, 1998, pp. 38–50.

Dawson, T., 'Klivanion revisited: an evolutionary typology and catalogue of middle Byzantine lamellar', *Journal of Roman Military Equipment Studies*, 12/13, 2001/02, pp. 11–24.

Dawson, T., 'Suntagma Hoplôn: the equipment of regular Byzantine troops, c. 950–c.1204', in David Nicolle (ed.), *Companion to Medieval Arms and Armour* (London: Boydell & Brewer, 2002, pp. 81–90).

Dawson, T., *One Thousand Years of Lamellar Construction in the Roman World* (Armidale: Levantia Guides no. 8, 2003, 2010).

Dawson, T., *Byzantine Infantryman: c.900–1204* (Oxford: Osprey, 2009).

Dawson, T., 'The Walpurgis Fechtbuch: an inheritance of Constantinople?', *Arms and Armour* (Leeds: Royal Armouries Museum, 2009).

Dawson, T., *Byzantine Cavalryman: c.900–1204* (Oxford: Osprey, 2009).

Dean, B., *Helmets and Body Armour in Modern Warfare* (New Haven, CT: Yale University Press, 1920).

Dean, B., 'The exploration of a Crusaders' fortress (Montfort) in Palestine', *The Bulletin of the Metropolitan Museum of Art New York*, vol. XXII, Sept. 1927, part II, pp. 5–46.

Delius, P. and Hattstein, M., *Islam: Art and Architecture* (Cologne, H.F. Ullmann, 2007).

Dennis, G.T. (trans.), *Maurice's Stratêgicon* (Philadelphia: University of Pennsylvania Press, 1984). See also Mavrikios.

Dennis, G.T. (ed. & trans.), *Three Byzantine Military Treatises* (Washington, DC: Dumbarton Oaks, 1985).

Dennis, G.T. (ed. & trans.), *The Taktika of Leo VI* (Washington, DC: Dumbarton Oaks, 2010).

Dobra, Z., Durdik, J. and Wagner, E., *Medieval Costume, Armour and Weapons* (Mineola, NY: Dover Publications, 2000).

Eliav, Y.Z., Friedland, E.A. and Herbert, S. (eds), *The Sculptural Environment of the Roman Near East: Reflections on Culture, Ideology, and Power* (Leuven: Peeters, 2008).

Elgood, R., *Islamic Arms and Armour* (London: Scholar Press, 1979).

Folda, J., *Crusader Art* (Aldershot, UK: Lund Humphries, 2008).

Gawlikowski, M., 'The Statues of the Sanctuary of Allat in Palmyra', in Eliav *et al.* (eds), *The Sculptural Environment of the Roman Near East*, pp. 395–411.

Gjerstad, E., Lindros, J., Sjoqvist, E. and Westholm, A., *The Swedish Cyprus Expedition: Finds and results of the excavations in Cyprus, 1927–1931* (Stockholm: Swedish Cyprus Expedition, 1934–48).

Glad, D., 'The empire's influence on barbarian elites from the Pontus to the Rhine (5th–7th centuries): A case study of lamellar weapons and segmental helmets', in Ivanišević, V. and Kazanski, M., *The Pontic-Danubian Realm in the Period of the Great Migration* (Paris: Centre de Recherche d'Histoire et Civilisation de Byzance, 2012).

Gonen, R., *Weapons of the Ancient World* (London: Cassell, 1975).

Gorelik, M., 'Arms and armour in south-eastern Europe in the second half of the first millennium AD', in Nicolle, D. (ed.), *Companion to Medieval Arms and Armour*, pp. 127–147.

Gorelik, M., 'Oriental armour of the Near and Middle East from the eighth to the fifteenth centuries as shown in works of art', in Robert Elgood (ed.), *Islamic Arms and Armour* (London: Scholar Press, 1979).

Gorelik, M., *The Battle of Kulikov 1380: Russian troops and the Golden Horde* (published in Russian as *Куликовская битва 1380 г.: русский и золотоордынский воины*), Moscow.

Grancsay, S.V., 'A Sassanian chieftain's helmet', *The Metropolitan Museum of Art Bulletin*, new series, vol. 21, no. 8, 1963, pp. 253–262.

Grant, A.J. (ed. & trans.), *Early Lives of Charlemagne by Eginhard and the Monk of St Gall* (London: Chatto & Windus, 1926, p. 146).

Gravett, C., *Medieval German Armies, 1000–1300* (Oxford: Osprey, 1997).

Grotowski, P.Ł., *Arms and Armour of the Warrior Saints* (Leiden: Brill, 2010).

Haldon, John, 'Some Aspects of Early Byzantine Arms and Armour', in Nicolle (ed.), *Companion to Medieval Arms and Armour*, pp. 65–79.

Hattstein and Delius (eds), *Islamic Art and Architecture* (Cologne: H.F. Ullmann, 2007).

Hillenbrand, R., *Islamic Art and Architecture* (London: Thames and Hudson, 1999).

Hoffmeier, J.K., 'Military', *The Oxford Encyclopaedia of Ancient Egypt, vol. II*, edited by Donald B. Redford (New York: Oxford University Press, 2001, pp. 400–12).

Howard-Davis, C., *et al.*, *The Carlisle Millennium Project: Excavations in Carlisle, 1998–2001, vol. 2 – The Finds* (Lancaster, UK: Oxford Archaeology North, 2009).

Hunger, Herbert, 'On the Imitation (ΜΙΜΗΣΙΣ) of Antiquity', Dumbarton Oaks Papers, 23–24, 1969–70, pp. 15–38.

James, S., *The Excavations at Dura-Europos conducted by Yale University and the French Academy of Inscriptions and Letters 1928–1937* (London: British Museum Press, 2004).

Jones, L., *Between Islam and Byzantium: Aght'amar and the Visual Construction of Medieval Armenian Rulership* (Aldershot, UK: Ashgate, 2007).

Kajiwara, H., 'On lamellae: Lamellar armour from a Eurasian viewpoint', *Tohoku*

Fukushi University Serizawa Keisuke Art and Craft Museum Annual Report, vol. 1, 2009, pp. 57–80.

Kennedy, H., *Armies of the Caliphs: Military and Society in the Early Islamic State* (London: Routledge, 2001).

Khorasani, M.M., *Arms and Armour from Iran: The Bronze Age to the End of the Qajar Period* (Tübingen, Legat-Verlag, 2006).

Khorasani, M.M., 'Linguistic terms describing different types of armour in Persian manuscripts', *Gladius*, XXXI, 2011, pp. 149–88.

Laking, G.F., *A Catalogue of the Arms and Armour in the Armoury of the Knights of St John of Jerusalem, now in the Palace, Valletta, Malta* (London: Agnew & Co., 1905; Huntingdon, UK: Ken Trotman, 2008).

Lazarev, V.N., 'A new painting from the twelfth century and the figure of St George the Warrior in Byzantine and medieval Russian art', in V. Lazarev, *Studies in Early Russian Art* (London, Pindar Press, 2000).

Lev, Y. (ed.), *War and Society in the Eastern Mediterranean, 7th–15th Centuries* (Leiden: Brill, 1996).

Lillie, Ralph-Johannes, *Byzantium and the Crusader States* (Oxford: Clarendon Press, 1993).

Makushnikov, O.L. and Lupinenko, Y.M., 'Lamellar armour of the Eastern Slav warrior of the beginning of the 13th century (according to the materials of Gomel excavations)', *Historical-Archaeological Studies*, 18, 2003.

Mavrikios, Emperor, *Das Strategikon des Maurikios*, edited by George T. Dennis and translated by Ernst Gamillscheg (Vienna: Verlag der Österreichischen Akademie der Wissenschaften, 1981).

May, A.F., *Der Schmuck aus jungpaläololithischen Bestattungen in Frankreich und Ligurien* (Berne: Fritz Marti, 1962).

McGeer, E., *Sowing the Dragon's Teeth: Byzantine Warfare in the Tenth Century* (Washington, DC: Dumbarton Oaks, 1995).

Michalak, A., 'Czy w średniowieczu na ziemiach polskich używano skśrzanych pancerzy?' (Was leather armour used on Polish lands in the Medieval period?), in Kucypery, P., Pudło, P. and Żabińskiego, G., *Arma et Medium Aevum Studia nad uzbrojeniem średniowiecznym* (Toruń, Adam Marszałek, 2010).

Negin, A.E. 'Sarmatian Cataphracts as prototypes for Roman *equites cataphractarii*', *Journal of Roman Military Equipment Studies*, vol. 9, 1998, pp. 65–75.

Nickel, H., 'The mutual influence of Europe and Asia in the field of arms and armour', in Nicolle, D. (ed.), *Companion to Medieval Arms and Armour*, 2002.

Nicolle, D., *Armies of Islam, 7th–11th Centuries* (Oxford: Osprey, 1982).

Nicolle, D., *The Crusades* (Oxford: Osprey, 1988).

Nicolle, D., *Arms and Armour of the Crusading Era, 1050–1350* (New York: Greenhill Books, 1988).

Nicolle, D., *Rome's Enemies 5: The Desert Frontier* (Oxford: Osprey, 1991).

Nicolle, D., 'Arms of the Umayyad Era', in Yaacov L. (ed.), *War and Society in the Eastern Mediterranean, 7th–15th Centuries*.

Nicolle, D., *Medieval Warfare Sourcebook, vol. 1: Warfare in Western Christendom*

(London: Arms and Armour Press, 1994).

Nicolle, D., *Medieval Warfare Sourcebook, vol. 2: Christian Europe and its Neighbours* (London: Arms and Armour Press, 1996).

Nicolle, D., *Companion to Medieval Arms and Armour* (Woodbridge: Boydell Press, 2002).

Nicolle, D., *Carolingian Cavalryman, AD 768–987* (Oxford: Osprey, 2005).

Paulsen, P., *Alamannische Adelsgraber von Niederstotzingen* (Stuttgart: Verlag Muller & Graff, 1967).

Pilipko, V.N., 'Arms and armours from Old Nisa', in Pilipko, V.N., Mode, M., Tubach, J. and Vashalomidze, G.S. (eds), *Arms and Armour as Indicators of Cultural Transfer: The Steppes and the Ancient World from Hellenistic Times to the Early Middle Ages* (Proceedings of the 'Nomaden und sesshafte' conference, Wittenberg, Germany, 2003) (Wiesbaden: Reichert, 2006, pp. 259–94).

Pirling, R., *Das Romisch-Fränkische Gräberfeld von Krefeld-Gellep, 1964–1965* (Berlin: Gebr. Mann Verlag, 1979).

Price, P., 'An interesting find of Lorica Plumata from the Roman fortress at Usk', in Bishop, M.C. (ed.), *Roman Military Equipment* (Proceedings of a seminar held in the Department of Ancient History and Classical Archaeology at the University of Sheffield, 21 March 1983) (Sheffield: University of Sheffield, 1983, pp. 12–13).

Pyhrr, S.W. and Godoy, J-A., *Heroic Armour of the Italian Renaissance: Filippo Negroli and His Contemporaries* (New York: New York Metropolitan Museum of Art, 1999).

Robinson, H.R., *Oriental Armour* (London: Herbert Jenkins, 1967).

Robinson, H.R., *The Armour of Imperial Rome* (London: Arms and Armour Press, 1975).

Rogers, H.C. and LaRocca, D., 'A New World find of European scale armour', *Gladius*, vol. XIX, 1999, pp. 221–30.

Sánchez, J.V., 'Early Byzantine lamellar armour from Carthago Spartaria (Cartgena)', *Gladius*, vol. XXVIII, 2008, pp. 195–210.

Sarnecki, W. and Nicolle, D., *Medieval Polish Armies: 966–1500* (Oxford: Osprey, 2008).

Siddorn, J.K., *Viking Weapons and Warfare* (Stroud, UK: Tempus, 2000).

Simkins, M., *The Roman Army from Hadrian to Constantine* (Oxford: Osprey, 1979).

Skinner, P., Tumanishvili, D. and Shanshiashvili, A. (eds), *The Caucasus: Georgia on the Crossroads. Cultural Exchanges Across Europe and Beyond* (Tbilisi: Georgian Arts and Culture Centre, 2011).

Snodgrass, A., *Early Greek Armour and Weapons from the End of the Bronze Age to 600 BC* (Edinburgh: Edinburgh University Press, 1964).

Stone, G.C., *A Glossary of the Construction, Decoration and Use of Arms and Armour in all Countries and in all Times, Together With Some Closely Related Subjects* (New York: Brussel, 1961).

Thordeman, B., *Armour from the Battle of Wisby, 1361* (Stockholm: Alqvist and Wiskell, 1938).

Travis, H. & Travis, J., *Roman Body Armour* (Stroud, UK: Amberley Publishing, 2012).

Treviño, R., *Rome's Enemies 4: Spanish Armies, 218–19 BC* (Oxford: Osprey, 1986).

Tsamakda, V., *The Illustrated Chronicle of the Ioannis Skylitzes in Madrid* (Leiden: Brill, 2002).

Tsurtsumia, M., 'The evolution of splint armour in Georgia and Byzantium, lamellar and scale armour in the 10th–12th centuries', *Byzantina Σymmeikta*, vol. 21, 2011, pp. 65–99.

Vdovin, V.Y. and Nikonorov, V.P., 'Fragments of armour of the late Sassanian period from Togolok-Depe', *Journal of the Turkmen SSR Academy of Sciences*, Humanities Series, no. 4 (1991), pp. 77–79.

Von Groller, M., 'Römische Waffen', *Der Römische Limes in Österreich*, 2, 1901, pp. 85–132.

Walter, C., *The Warrior Saints in Byzantine Art and Tradition* (Aldershot: Ashgate, 2003).

Whitcomb, D.S., 'Before the roses and nightingales: excavations at Qasr-i Abu Nasr, Old Shiraz', Metropolitan Museum of Art, New York, 1985.

Wiesehöfer, J., *Ancient Persia* (London: L.B. Tauris, 1996 (2001)).

Wijnhoven, M.A., '*Lorica Hamata Squamataque*: A Study of Roman Hybrid Armour', *Journal of the Mail Research Society*, vol. 2 no. 1), 2009, pp. 3–29.

Wijnhoven, M.A., 'The Ouddorp Lorica: A Case Study of Roman *Lorica Hamata Squamataque*', *Journal of the Mail Research Society*, vol. 2 (no. 1), 2009, pp. 30–65.

Wilcox, P., *Rome's Enemies 3: Parthians and Sassanid Persians* (Oxford: Osprey, 1986).

Williams, A., *The Sword and the Crucible: A History of the Metallurgy of European Swords up to the 16th Century* (Leiden: Brill, 2012).

Wilson, N.G., 'The Madrid Skylitzes', *Scrittura e Civilita*, vol. 2, 1978, pp. 209–19.

Wise, T., *Ancient Armies of the Middle East* (Oxford: Osprey, 1987).

Zijlstra-Zweens, H.M., *Of His Array Telle I No Lenger Tale: Aspects of Costume, Arms and Armour in Western Europe, 1200–1400* (Amsterdam: Rodopi, 1988).

INDEX

If you enjoyed this book, you may also be interested in...

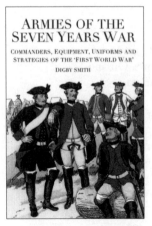

Armies of the Seven Years War: Commanders, Equipment, Uniforms and Strategies of the 'First World War'

Digby Smith

Drawn from many international sources, Armies of the Seven Years War is the finest reference work on this most complex of conflicts. It details the senior commanders, uniforms, weapons, equipment, artillery, strategy and tactics (military and naval) of the forces that fought – in effect – for world supremacy from 1756 to 1763.

978 0 7524 9214 8

British Napoleonic Field Artillery: The First Complete Illustrated Guide to Equipment and Uniforms

C.E. Franklin

This beautifully illustrated guide draws together extensive research to provide a new insight into the field artillery and uniforms of the Napoleonic Wars. The evolution of this new form of artillery is shown in full detail for the first time, and its use is fully examined. Particular attention is given to the ammunition, drills, harness, supporting equipment and uniforms of the period, and each type of field artillery is fully illustrated.

978 0 7524 7652 0

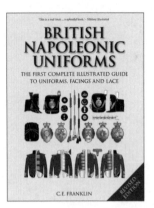

British Napoleonic Uniforms: The First Complete Illustrated Guide to Uniforms, Facings and Lace

C.E. Franklin

For the first time, a book discusses and illustrates in colour the change in uniforms, the colour of the facings and the nature and shape of the lace for the officers, NCOs and private soldiers of the numbered regiments of cavalry and infantry over the period of the Napoleonic War. This revised edition has been updated and a colour guide specifically for modellers has been added.

978 1 8622 7484 6

Visit our website and discover thousands of other History Press books.

www.thehistorypress.co.uk